JOHN WINTERS

Entrepreneurship

Copyright © 2018 by John Winters

All rights reserved. No part of this publication may be reproduced, stored or transmitted in any form or by any means, electronic, mechanical, photocopying, recording, scanning, or otherwise without written permission from the publisher. It is illegal to copy this book, post it to a website, or distribute it by any other means without permission.

First edition

This book was professionally typeset on Reedsy.
Find out more at reedsy.com

Contents

Introduction — iv
What is Entrepreneurship? — 1
How to Become an Entrepreneur — 6
Entrepreneurship Success — 10
The Common Mistakes that First Time Entrepreneurs Must... — 18
The 5 Skills of a Good Entrepreneur — 21
The Startup Business — 37
Online Entrepreneurship — 53
Social Media Marketing For Online Businesses — 82
Lifestyle Design — 98
Conclusion — 110

Introduction

Good entrepreneurs are the artists of the modern world. They take ideas and create remarkable products and services. They can take an empty canvas and create things that seemed impossible.

Steve Jobs is probably one of the most talked about entrepreneurs of our time.He revolutionized the way we look at technology!He made browsing the internet an artistic experience.If you ever had an iPad or Apple product in your hand, then you would know what I mean. Apple products are special and unique. Now it's one of the biggest and cutting edge companies in the world. They made magic out of nothing.

The important thing to remember is that Apple started out as an idea in someone's bedroom.Steve Jobs was a normal guy and with the help of a couple of friends they started something remarkable that changed the world.

You have the same opportunity to create something remarkable. You can take your ideas and create your vision. Today people have more resources than any other time in history.The internet has made knowledge freely available and has created massive opportunities.

Sure, becoming an entrepreneur is not easy. There are risks involved. The path might be filled with disappointments, but if you persevere and work hard, then success is yours for the taking.

The world is changing, and more brave people are taking the big step and becoming entrepreneurs. The traditional path of working for 30 years and retiring is becoming outdated.

If you are thinking of becoming an entrepreneur, then it means you are different, brave and willing to walk the path less traveled.

I hope you enjoy this book, and that it inspires and helps you to take the next step in becoming an entrepreneur.

Good Luck!

1

What is Entrepreneurship ?

Entrepreneurship is the process of building a business venture from scratch. More than that, it is a way of life. The path of the entrepreneur has been taken by many famous individuals like Bill Gates, Elon Musk, Mark Zuckerberg, and Richard Branson among others. These people have brought significant contributions to the world, by creating new things and defying the status quo.

Entrepreneurship is a lifestyle combined with the passion of learning new things, creating answers to problems, leading people towards a positive goal, and giving value to the world. Many of today's advancements have been brought by entrepreneurs and innovative thinkers. These people who have dared to be different and took on a great amount of risk are the reasons why the world is a better place to live in.

Entrepreneurship as an Alternative Career Option

Still, not everything in the world is as perfect as many expect them to be. In several economies, the outlook is grim as there are fewer jobs offered to people. The opportunities for employment and gain become smaller each day. Instead of depending on big companies and corporate firms, you can start small and build your own enterprise. Entrepreneurship is a great alternative which can give you fulfillment in seeing your prized idea come to life.

It seems that entrepreneurship is becoming more popular nowadays. More fresh graduates, for example, are starting their own food businesses instead of joining the ranks of corporate organizations. News and magazine interviews tell of younger individuals who eventually made millions from a business they started out as hobbies on top of their education. Of course, who can forget about those who have dropped out of school to pursue something bigger than a diploma? People like Steve Jobs have done this, and now he is considered a legend.

Entrepreneurship requires no age restriction. You can start even if you are in your late 30s, 40s, or 50s. Colonel Sanders of Kentucky Fried Chicken fame had the idea for his business when he was 65. The only requirement needed to pursue a business venture is the willingness to start.

The Benefits of Entrepreneurship to the Human Spirit

Once you become an entrepreneur, there is no going back to the office or being an employee of a big firm. You will now crave for freedom and creativity to run your own venture. Here are just some of the benefits that entrepreneurs get in being their own boss.

1. The Freedom to Follow One's Own Voice

Instead of following your boss' instructions, you become free to follow your own wishes. You can do anything you want. You have the power to work when you want to, and stop when you feel like it. Your ideas become of great importance as you embark in entrepreneurship to make your ambitions happen.

2. Control of One's Time and Flexibility

Time is the greatest treasure of all, not money. When you control your own time, you are controlling your own destiny. Unfortunately, employees do not have a say on how to manage this valuable resource. They have to be at the beck and call of their superiors, which is not exactly one of the best feelings in the world.

3. Excitement

Every day in the life of an entrepreneur is a challenge. No two days are the same. On some days, you will be earning a lot, and then the next few months could carry a dry spell. If you dislike routine, then you are going to like the career path of an entrepreneur for its variety and propensity for excitement.

4. Pride in Achieving Goals

As an entrepreneur, you dictate your own goals. You will acquire a sense of pride in accomplishing your dreams and making things happen. It would also be sweeter to achieve since you will pass through difficulties first before earning success.

5. A Chance to Learn New Things

You have the ability to learn things you are deeply interested in, as well as in topics you would rather skip. As an entrepreneur, you have to be well-rounded in knowing all the possibilities to aptly prepare for potential problems. Learning new knowledge will give you the edge needed in running the business.

6. Limitless Earnings

An employee would have a fixed salary, while entrepreneurs do not. Part of the sacrifices you have to make is to throw job security out the window. From now on, you don't have a limit to how much you earn. Every income you will get is a direct result of your efforts and a few strokes of luck.

7. Building Self Esteem

The more an entrepreneur builds a bigger and stronger enterprise, the more his confidence in himself grows. Entrepreneurs are also known as nicer bosses since they have a relatively kinder approach in handling stress.

8. The Opportunity to Get the Full Reward

The full reward may include huge income, media coverage, or simply the joy in living out your dreams and being successful at it. As an entrepreneur, you are entitled to the full rewards of your efforts since each day is a challenge well fought.

The Benefits of Entrepreneurship to the Community

The advantages of entrepreneurship do not end with the individuals who have taken the risk of establishing their own enterprise. Its benefits extend up to the community which they help as a result of their efforts.

1. Generating New Jobs

Small to medium enterprises help communities by providing jobs to the locals. Entrepreneurs become more engaged with the community they live in by making a direct impact in the lives of their people. In times of economic difficulties, entrepreneurs help people earn money by making use of their skills to achieve the goals of the business.

2. Creating an Impact to the Economy

Businesses drive the lifeblood of the economy. They stimulate activity and give value to the total domestic income of the country. There are more benefits as well when citizens decide to support local businesses. Incomes get higher, and people generally become happier.

3. Provide Solutions to Problems

Lastly, entrepreneurship provides answers. They create value which people pay for to solve their problems. This opportunity is a rare one which can only be started by creative minds keen on building their own business. If you want to make the world a better place, start by finding a problem which you can solve and exchange for value.

2

How to Become an Entrepreneur

Becoming an entrepreneur is a mixture of science and art. You need plans to form the logic part of the business. This includes setting up shop, offering a product or a service, and attaining business quotas to generate income. At the same time, running a business is an art form. You need to understand the inner workings of the mind of your customers to become profitable.

Identify a Niche

Before starting a business venture, settle on a niche which you will serve. Focus on that area and center your products and services based on what the niche requires. For example, you want to open a restaurant. Decide first what kind of food you will serve your customers. Will it be healthy dishes, seafood meals, fast-food fare, or dessert items?

Write a Business Plan

The business plan is one of the most important resources of an entrepreneur. The plan highlights your vision, your mission, the goals of your business, and the financial projections needed by the business to stay afloat. Investors also require seeing the business plan before they decide to lend you money for capital in starting up shop.

However, I want to contradict myself a bit here.A business plan is not everything.I have started several businesses without one.But in hindsight, a business plan does give you direction and a roadmap so you can follow your progress and make sure you are becoming successful.

Offer Value for a Product or Service

The nature of your business' existence lies in the products and services you will offer to your market. Don't just offer what people need or want, create value that will justify the price and the usability of your products and services. Better yet, invent of an edge that will make your business a more attractive choice over competitors.

Pinpoint a Target Market

Your niche screens the potential consumers of your products and services. If you are serving healthy options for lunch, then that means you are ruling out people looking for fried food items as potential customers. It's impossible to attract everybody because that will mean your business does not have a brand which to identify with. Focus on your primary markets and refine offerings to cater to the taste of your targets.

Do Research

Relying on gut feel is one thing. At some points in running your business, you will encounter occasions where you are forced to decide on the spot. On these events, using your instincts is wise and recommended. But for the other aspects of the business, you should rely on research and calculated guesses. Do research as to what kind of items or services your target market will like and probably pay for. Never assume. Base your decisions on the data you have collected in refining the offerings and price points of your business.

Build a Startup

The ultimate test that an entrepreneur will face includes building the startup business from the ground up. You, as the head of the business venture, will face several difficulties and losing streaks of luck before you reach the line of success. Consider your new startup as your own child. Treat it with care and attention, but be objective enough to acknowledge shortcomings. Be flexible in running operations yet remain firm in your decisions. Allow for space in making mistakes. Learn the ropes of steering the business in profitable directions. You will get to success eventually if you play your cards right.

Handle Your Finances

Handling money correctly is perhaps the most underrated advice entrepreneurs receive when asking for tips on how to successfully build a business. Never underestimate the power of money. Most businesses fail in the first few years because the managers practice incorrect ways in handling the cash flows. If you want your business to succeed, you have to know where each cent goes. Manage the cash flow well and prevent unnecessary expenses from eating up your business' capital.

Last Piece of Advice: Take a Stand

As mentioned, entrepreneurship is a lifestyle. It's beyond the path of having a career; it extends into your personal life as well. In this line of thought, be prepared to fight naysayers if you truly want to succeed. You will encounter many of them as you climb up and accomplish milestones in your chosen career.

A tip is to be persistent. Take a stand from unsupportive circles like skeptic family members and friends. Learn how to focus your efforts effectively and never take your eyes from the prize. Lastly, persevere and never give up. You will find that you are closer to success the greater your problems become, so just keep on going. You will get there eventually.

3

Entrepreneurship Success

Entrepreneurship is defined as a way of thinking, reasoning, and acting. This is according to Jeffrey Timmons, in his book New Venture Creation. It is more than just having the talent and skills, it needs to be properly and strategically planned, it also requires passion and discipline to build a business that will last and you will enjoy doing. That is just some of the characteristics an individual must have to attain entrepreneurship success.

An entrepreneur is an individual who operates, manages, and controls a business in having the goal to earn profit. And to reach his goals, he must have these traits and attitudes:

1. Be Passionate

Passion is an important ingredient to achieve success. This will take you to the highest of your potential to reach your goals.

Do your best and you will exceed your limits as an entrepreneur. And to do your best, you must love what you are doing. Having no passion for work will just result to laziness and procrastination. If that happens, you'll never complete or attain your goals.

2. Be Disciplined

You need to focus on your goals, so that you can accomplish things needed in your business. If not, you will need to make more time to repair the damages or spend more time to finish your products or services.

There may also be changes from time to time about the demands of your customers and your capacity to work with it. It can give you stress that's why you also need to be flexible. Whatever changes that might happen in your business, you must be able to cope up with it.

3. Be a Risk-taker

As an entrepreneur, you must risk a lot of things especially money in starting your business. You must forget your fears and face the opportunities with confidence. From the start, you must know the risks that you will face in your chosen venture.

If you want to be more creative and innovative in your business, you must take risks to achieve a better result and higher entrepreneurship success.

4. Be a Trooper

A trooper is someone who exhibits extreme perseverance. To achieve entrepreneur success, "Never give up." Putting up a business is easy but managing and handling it is a different story. You must face challenges, problems, risks, and shortcomings but these are normal. The secret is perseverance. Whatever circumstances you meet along the way, never give up.

Everyone has the talent and skills to start his own business but not everyone can be an entrepreneur. You must have these entrepreneur attitudes to reach entrepreneurship success.

Success Secrets from Business Experts

Many business owners are often asked questions about the secrets to their company's success. Many of their replies would include things like having passion for the kind of work that you do or working extra hard at achieving your dreams.

While these pieces of advice are useful and very much true, some people might want to get answers that are a little bit more specific. The truth is that the secret of success is not just one exact event or action from your end but a series of positive actions and a bit of luck. One thing is for sure: it will take a lot of hard work in order for you to succeed. Only a few hundred people were able to succeed in life instantly. Everyone else, even the owners of big companies today, started out small and worked their way into becoming the great business experts that they are today.

It's Really Not a Secret

Many experts in business and successful business owners would often tell you that there really are no secrets of success in business. They would tell you that everything you need to succeed is all in you. It is in your head, in your heart, and in your entire being. This means that you have to have the right mindset and attitude in order to truly succeed in life.

Another thing that successful entrepreneurs would tell you about the secret of their success is that most of their success can be attributed to great ideas, stellar teams, and support from friends and family. If you have all of this, does that mean that you will succeed? The answer is both yes and no. It can be a yes if you do the right things and make the right decisions. It can be a no if you do not do anything about that great idea.

Some successful entrepreneurs would also say that their success is a result of a lot of luck. The truly lucky ones are those who have a good life already handed to them. These are also the people who have the right businesses at the right time. People who succeed in life through luck are those who get a sudden windfall of cash and are able to turn it into something bigger.

So There's No Secret???

Of course there is! But the secret to succeeding in business is not really something that you do not know. In most cases, people already know these not-so-secret tips but do not regularly get to apply them in their daily lives.

Take a look at these tips:

Keep trying even if you fail -

Whether you like it or not, failure and success sometimes go hand in hand. Some people would never experience failure while others would fail repeatedly before they can succeed. The secret here is to keep trying. If you truly believe that your idea has merit, do not give up on it. Tweak your idea until it becomes perfect. Do not accept no for an answer.

Many successful business ideas were rejected several times before they became a success. Some of the most successful people like Jack Ma of Alibaba, for example, applied for admission to Harvard and was rejected 10 times before he was able to get in. He now owns one of the largest retail sites in the world.

Work hard –

This advice is very cliché for most people but it is still true nonetheless.

Most successful businesses succeed because their owners worked more than anyone in the company. This often applies to startup companies that have very little manpower to help them get their businesses running.

Working hard means that you are the salesperson, the idea person, the executive, the designer, and sometimes the messenger and delivery person all rolled into one. You have to be ready to take on any kind of task and role in order to succeed. No position is too lowly for anyone who wants to succeed. If you need someone to clean up the mess and do the dirty work, you have to be ready to do it yourself.

Do your research –

90% of the time, good businesses fail because the owners did not do enough research about their product, their market, their competition, and everything that has to do with their business. People who make businesses out of trends and fleeting fads are great examples of people who do not do enough research. They simply go with the bandwagon and hope that their business would take off.

This is not to say that trends cannot become good businesses. People who strike while the iron is hot can still make a ton of money with these businesses. Even if they do not do enough research, the money could still come in simply because these things are in demand. It's a great way to start their business. The research can come later.

Have a good backup system -

While it is true that you can never really plan for everything, having a good backup system will save you tons of money, time, and effort. Make sure that whatever you do, you always have a good fallback, or backup system in case something fails. Diversify your product offerings so that if one does not sell, you still have something else to sell and derive income from. You can also try venturing into a completely different business in order to truly diversify your portfolio. If you are in the restaurant business, for example, try another completely unrelated field like construction or transportation. It might mean that more capital will be needed but it also means that if one of them fails or if you encounter a snag in one of your businesses, the other can easily help keep the other afloat.

Learn from your mistakes – failing hurts.

But it also teaches you a good lesson about your business. Do not be afraid of failure. It will only make you a better businessman if you have experienced what failure feels like. Try to minimize the risk of failure by referring to item #4 and diversifying your businesses. If the idea of failure really terrifies you, you can try getting inspiration from others who have failed and learn from them. Read biographies, personal success stories, and find out how successful people have overcome their trials.

Learn to adapt to changes –

Change is as inevitable as death. You must be willing to go with the changes that your business encounters or risk becoming stagnant and obsolete. Nokia is a good example of this. Nokia used to be the best mobile phone company with billions in revenue for more than a decade. But when smartphone companies started popping up, they stuck with their old phone designs and soon their revenue dropped. Smartphones and other touch screen devices are now reaping the profits that Nokia once had. Being able to adapt to change also means that you have the capacity, the technology, and the know-how. Make sure to keep yourself updated with the latest trends and business practices.

Never stop learning –

One of the most common traits that all successful businessmen have is their unwavering thirst for learning. Even after they have graduated from Ivy League schools and earned their MBAs, successful people never think that they know everything. They would often read and keep up with the latest news and trends. They would try to discover new places and new way of doing things if they feel that this is something that could add value to their businesses. Successful people are always asking questions and wondering about how the world works. They do not shy away from trying new things and trying new technology. They thrive in changes in society and the organization that they work with.

Think positive –

The power of the mind is truly amazing. You can actually will your success or at least make it easier for you to achieve success simply by picturing yourself as successful. This is very hard to believe for some but it is truly possible. How it works may sound like some cuckoo mumbo jumbo but it isn't. The way it works is by picturing in your mind that you have already achieved the success that you crave, your mind will start directing your body to replicate that thought and translate it to reality. Yep, your mind is that powerful.

The power of visualization and positive thinking are your mind's way of easing you into the tough tasks that you will encounter. By visualizing that you have already succeeded, your mind will start to think that every tough thing that you encounter can be conquered.

Make small attainable goals and big amazing goals –

Small attainable goals will help you feel like you are moving forward. Each small achievement gives you something to be proud of. Make small attainable goals in short timelines and work towards your big end goals. This helps you plan out your business strategies and help give you direction.

Create big goals that will help measure your success. Big goals like reaching the 1 Million sales mark or opening a new branch are milestone goals. Make goals big but attainable. Set a good timeline like 3 years for 1 Million sales. Use projections and other forecasting tools to help you determine how much farther you have to work before you achieve your goals.

Reward yourself –

All work and no play makes your life dull. Reward yourself when you reach a significant goal that you aimed for. Go on a vacation every once in a while. Unwind and relax with a good massage or a trip to the beach. Rewarding yourself in this manner helps keep your mind and ideas fresh. It also rejuvenates and energizes you so that you can be ready to take on new challenges.

You do not have to just be an awed admirer of the world's most successful businessmen. You too can be successful in your own craft, field, or expertise. Incorporate these success secrets in your own daily life and be on the same path to success.

4

The Common Mistakes that First Time Entrepreneurs Must Avoid

You will make mistakes. As a person, making mistakes is a normal part of life. The same goes with being an entrepreneur. You are alone in this venture, and you are the lone decision maker as well. Opportunities will present you plenty of events to test your will and determination. Some of these common mistakes are avoidable though.

Picking the Wrong Partner/s

Choose to associate with people who can contribute something different to the group. When it comes to traits, pick people who support what you do. Do not choose friends who will abandon you the moment circumstances get tough. Being stuck with the wrong kinds of people will become the death of your business.

Always Asking for Help

It might occur that you don't have the slightest idea in running a business. In these times, it's okay to ask for guidance from people who had years of experience in running successful enterprises. However, learn to be independent and seek answers on your own. Asking for help a few times wouldn't hurt, but don't commit the mistake of letting other people run your business for you. You still have to call the shots.

Not Asking for Help When You Need It

Of course, you should also know when to bring people in to solve problems beyond your abilities. During these times, it is crucial to let experts have their say so that you don't thrash the business to the ground. The last thing you want to do as a business owner is to be arrogant and to be blind to the problems of your firm. If you let your ego take over, your business might find it hard to recover from its losses.

Hiring the Wrong People

One of the most difficult parts of running a business includes managing people. As an entrepreneur, you have to be vigilant in hiring the right kinds of talents and personality traits to work for you. The wrong kind of people will drive your business down, no matter how great your products or services are. Learn to reward individuals who do their best work. It will increase morale and rapport between you and your employees. Of course, know when to let go of incompetent workers in your business as well.

Obsessing on Your Competition

Allowing yourself to check up on rivals from time to time is okay. But be wary; always thinking of ways to sabotage your competitors may take a toll on your decision-making efforts. Learn to be a fair player. Focus on creating great product offerings, refining services, and adding more value to your business rather than thinking of ways to simply get ahead.

Putting the Customer Last

The most important opinions you must take into consideration belong to your customers. Forget about what your family, friends, or investors say. Make your customers your priority. After all, they are the lifeblood of your business. When researching for the tastes and preferences of your market, go directly to the customers to get data for your business offerings. Never assume unless you have reliable data in your hands.

Running a Bootstrap Operation

Most entrepreneurs are guilty of running bootstrap operations. While the intentions are good, running tight operations might hurt the business venture for it does not allow room for error. Your employees will always have to strive to reach quotas just to make the business float.

It is all about prudence. You know you will make mistakes in your first year. If you have just enough cash to fund each month, you will get in trouble the soonest you fail to reach sales targets. Having enough money in the bank will also help you cushion the fall of low sales expectations.

Getting Too Attached to the Business

It is understandable to feel a close affinity to a business you have built from scratch. However, getting too attached might wreak more havoc than actual advantages for the business. If you get too attached, you will lose your objectivity. Decisions will be clouded with bias and partiality. You can prevent yourself from doing this by asking for feedback regularly. Have someone dependable to tell you the state of your business as is. Lastly, be flexible and gear up for change when the need arises.

5

The 5 Skills of a Good Entrepreneur

What makes up a good entrepreneur? What are the skills that good entrepreneurs possess? How can these skills be improved? How vital are these skills when it comes to running a business? These are the core questions that we will seek to answer at the end of this book.

We know that being an entrepreneur takes more than just spending money on building a business. It is more than being a boss. Being an entrepreneur is all about creating a culture of values that will lead both the company and the people towards the achievement of personal and corporate goals. An entrepreneur is not only responsible for the business, but he or she is also responsible for the lives of his employees.

A good entrepreneur is not only after profit. Providing lasting customer value is equally important to him. Now what are the 5 skills that make up a good entrepreneur?

- Creativity

- Good working standards

- Creation of product value

- Marketing

- Leadership

It is easy to become an entrepreneur. You just need money that you can invest in your chosen business venture and people to work for you. Once you have these two plus a business permit, you can already call yourself an entrepreneur. However, a good entrepreneur is like a pearl. It takes years of practice and commitment to company policies and goals.

Good entrepreneurs do not only reap a lot of profits but they also earn the trust and loyalty of their employees and customers. Good entrepreneurs create good brands that can last for generations.

The business industry is a wild world and if you are not a good entrepreneur, you will not survive in the wild. Good entrepreneurs know how to deal with people and they take care of people. They know that to be able to stay in the business, they should set priorities and take a lot of risks.

Are you an entrepreneur or a good entrepreneur? Let's find out...

Skill 1

Creativity: Why does it Matter to Good Entrepreneurs?

What is the most essential trait of a good entrepreneur? Many people will definitely claim that leadership is the most important trait of an entrepreneur. Leadership guides the people and the company towards success. Some people will also argue that passion is the most important trait for without passion, success will not be possible. However, others believe that creativity is the most important of them all. Creating possibilities and innovation makes a company stable and creativity makes it possible. A creative mind knows no boundaries and seeing the world in a different light is crucial to company's success.

Why is creativity important to good entrepreneurs?

Creativity is important for so many reasons. These are:

1. Creativity is acquired not born with: People say that artists are born with artistic talents. Yes, it is true. People are born with innate talents. However, creativity is not only about art. It is about making possibilities happen out of nothing. It is about constant innovation through one's imagination. Everyone has the potential to be creative. The mind is so powerful that it can be strengthened and improved.

Creative minds do not break in times of adversity. Instead, they make solutions to problems. Creative people know that there are always 6 ways out of a box. They will not stand there and wait for someone to rescue them. They will try as many possible solutions as they can and only then can they find the best solution to the problem and use it.

2. Creativity is better than intelligence: Most people have this connotation that if a person is intelligent, he has a higher chance of being successful in life. The truth is, intelligence is for the employees to possess and not for good entrepreneurs. What does it mean?

Success is not determined by how intelligent you are as a person. No matter how intelligent you are, if you are not creative, nothing will come out of your mind. Your ideas will remain ideas. However, if you are creative, your ideas will become reality. So intelligence is only for the employees...creativity is for entrepreneurs...because good entrepreneurs make things happen. This, however, does not mean that you don't need intelligence, no. As a matter of fact, creativity is a sign of intelligence so if you are creative, you are also intelligent. Intelligence is not only reflected in the academic achievements but also on how a person solves a problem at hand.

3. Creativity is divergence and convergence combined: A divergent mind has the ability to explore numerous possibilities for problem-solving. A convergent mind, on the other hand, focuses and analyzes the best solution to the problem. To be creative, one needs to look beyond the obvious. There are many ways to solve a problem but a good entrepreneur sees the best solution and he does it.

How to improve creativity:

There are a lot of ways for a person to improve his creativity:

1. Enhance your imagination - Imagination is the first step to innovation. Creating something out of nothing does not happen in just one click. One needs to form an idea and then make it a reality so in order to create something of value, an entrepreneur needs to have a very good imagination.

2. Visualize - All successful entrepreneurs and business tycoons believe that visualization led them to where they are now. Visualizing how your future will be makes it easier for you to focus on your goals and achieve them. Without a vision, a company will not be able to prosper.

3. Experiment on different strategies on how to complete a specific project - One strategy is not always enough to complete a project. There is always a better strategy to use and a good entrepreneur knows which strategy works best for a specific project.

4. Train your mind to be constantly active by doing mind
    -enriching activities like cross-word puzzles, Sudoku, word games etc. If the mind is constantly active, it remains sharp. However, it is also important to rest your mind once in a while; otherwise, you will burn yourself out and you will not be able to perform effectively.

5. Learn to recognize usual patterns in unusual objects put together.

Skill 2

Work Ethics: Getting Things Done

A good entrepreneur should have good working standards, period.
When we say ethics, whether it is medicine, law, business or any other professional disciplines, it is always defined as a set of standards governing the norms of society. Ethics is derived from universal set of values; thus, it starts in the most basic unit of society which is the family. Good entrepreneurs were taught at a very young age the importance of moral values.

In school, they learned to cultivate these values and incorporate them in their lives. These values are: trust and honesty, service and respect for others, loyalty and truth, justice and wisdom, moderation and prudence.

In business, good work ethics becomes a clash of moral values. Ethics in business is not only a philosophical concept. It always requires an action. Entrepreneurs need to do things - the right things. However, there are times, when the right thing to do means bending the law. For example, a business owner chooses to bribe to obtain a business contract just so his workers will still have a job. No business contract means no profit and that means laying-off a number of workers.

It is certainly not right to bribe but is laying-off some workers better? In business, ethics is not merely concerned about what is right and what is wrong. It is more of a consciousness about business obligations, human values and moral standards.

How to Attain Good Work Ethics?

1. Set priorities: For a business to keep on running, the owner must set priorities based in the order of importance and not in the sense of urgency. Learning to identify the most important aspects of the business makes it easier to manage business concerns. Do not give in to urgency but learn to treat important matters urgently.

2. Communicate and align personal and corporate goals: Corporate goals should be communicated properly and must be effectively understood by both the employees and business owners. These goals should also be aligned to one's personal goals to ensure personal growth and success within the company.

3. Ensure balance between work and life: Good working standards call for a balance between one's personal life and career. Some people focus on building and stabilizing their career that they forget what's more important in their life. There are people who fell in love so deeply with their work that they have forgotten what it's like to go out and have fun. Good entrepreneurs have time for their business and they still see to it that they have quality time with their families and loved ones.

4. Strive for excellence: Every good entrepreneur aims to achieve

excellence. It is not enough to perform if it is possible to be on top. Good entrepreneurs strive for excellence because they don't want their company to be just "average". Good work ethics requires an entrepreneur to beat their competition. Customers crave for excellence and if the company is not good enough, customer loyalty will be difficult to establish. Excellence makes successful brands.

Skill 3

Creating Value with Products

Whenever we attend company meetings and conferences, we always hear the word "product value". This, however, does not only refer to the product price per se, but it also entails the quality of the product and how customers perceive its value.

Sales talk is boring to customers if they cannot see the real value of the product. The sales agent should not just talk about the features of their product and services but more importantly, they should also strive to create a connection between the benefits of their products and services to the needs of the customers. Good sales people know how to position the company's products and services in such a way that the customer will see the value of the product, thereby motivating them to buy it.

When a customer sees the product value, price becomes less important. That is why most reliable companies and most stable brands are not really that cheap because their product value surpassed their product price.

How to create product value?

1. Know the customers: When it comes to product value, customers are the most important factors to consider. A good and successful entrepreneur knows his customers. He knows what his customers are looking for and what his customers' needs are. Before an entrepreneur can launch a product or service, he should already know his target market.

He should be able to get inside their customer's head and perceive what they value. By understanding and perceiving the customer value, the business owner can make specific strategies and tactics on how to lure customers to patronize his products and services. People have different needs and wants but a good and successful entrepreneur sees the common interest.

2. Establish rapport: If you want to know what customers really value, knowing them is not enough. One should be able to build a connection and only then a customer will open up. In the sales industry, the sales clerk builds a strong connection with the customer in order to gain a customer's trust. Building rapport is never easy though. Customers are too smart to know that you are just after sales conversion.

To build rapport, it is important to learn how to empathize. This way, you understand what the customer is going through and from there, you can position the "solutions" to your customer problems by incorporating your products and services.

3. Build lasting value: Building a lasting product value is easier said than done, but what really matters is that the customers see the importance of the product and what it can do to improve their life. Customers look for proof, so you need to be ready to show some proof on how effective your products and services are. You also need to bear in mind that each customer is different, so a different approach is always necessary.

These are the things that you need to remember to build lasting product value:
- Know the situation your customers are in,
- How strong the relationships among your buying team,
- The right questions to ask,
- The customer's lifestyles
- And their ability to tolerate changes.

Skill 4

Mastering the Art of Marketing and Sales

Good entrepreneurs know the importance of marketing. Some business owners are not very excited about promoting their products because they think selling themselves to the customers is embarrassing. Well, if you have a lot of money, you can just hire a marketing company and let them do the work for you. That is why a lot of marketing agencies are hired by big companies whenever they need to do a product launch.

However, if you are just starting to build your own business, you need to do all the marketing jobs yourself and without promotion, your business is just a name and a website without profit...

Here are the three important things you need to consider to ensure that marketing leads to product sales and customer value:

1. Business objectives: Before marketing your product, ask yourself first "what do you aim to achieve with your products and services?" What is your goal? Do you want to be known for product quality? Do you want your customers to see your company as a company that sells

stylish products with good quality and affordable prices? Do you aim to make the business running for a long time or is it just for this season? You need to ask yourself these questions before you can really target a specific audience.

2. Who are your customers: After deciding and enumerating your company's objectives, you need to identify your target market. Who are your target customers? Is it the female population? Is it the students? Do you want to cater to vegetarians? Do you want to focus on real estate development? Are you into sales of ladies apparel? Do you prefer to focus on musical instruments? Are you more of an expert in pharmacy?

You see, there are a lot of possible markets out there. It depends on which market you are going to focus on. Some entrepreneurs believe that targeting multiple markets in just one blow gives the company more chances of generating huge profits. The truth is, the more focused your target market is, the more stable your income gets. You want your company to be known for something.

For example, if you want to be known as the best sushi place in town, then you better focus on making sushi. If you want to be the best vegetarian restaurant, then strive to improve your vegetarian menus on a daily basis. That does not mean you can't innovate. Focusing on one's specialty makes a lot of room for innovations.

3. How can you generate profits? Business should lead to profits all the time. If you are not making money, then you are not running a business. You are merely doing something like a hobby. In order to master the art of marketing, you need to know ways to generate profits. Marketing can surely bring you sales but without an appropriate platform to launch the product, your target audience will not be able to find you.

It is best to use social media platforms and print advertisements like magazines and broadsheets. Billboards are really effective, and flyers can go a long way. Once you have considered these three factors, your business will surely prosper.

10 Reasons Why You Should Learn Sales

"Don't go to work to work, go to work to prosper," is the advice of Grant Cardone. Cardone graduated college set on a career in accounting but then changed course to work in automobile sales. He didn't believe himself to be a salesperson, but he persevered and made himself one. Now, he has seven best-selling books on sales, is a successful real estate investor and entrepreneur, and is a celebrated motivational speaker and trainer. His story is the perfect example to show that anyone can be a sales expert with commitment and hard work.

Sales is a field that most people are hesitant to venture into, due to the misconception that because they don't have the natural ability to sell, they will never succeed. The truth is, selling is not an innate talent; it is a skill that you can learn and practice. You don't need to have a marketing degree or business background; anyone can be a salesperson with the right mindset – that is, a commitment to hard work, pushing boundaries, and constant learning.

Here are ten reasons why learning how to sell is important not just to make money and get rich, but to grow as a person:

1. You gain confidence.
Salespeople always sound like they know what they're talking about. They make you believe in and trust what they're saying. You may not be naturally confident, but as you continue your selling endeavors, you will slowly become more and more confident with your knowledge about the product or service you're selling, with your understanding of your

potential customer or client, and with your ability as a salesperson. Until then, fake it till you make it.

2. You understand people better.

A bit of psychology is always involved in selling, because you are dealing with people. You have to figure out people's wants, needs, and problems – which sometimes they don't even realize yet themselves – and you have to be able to offer solutions, as well as be able to communicate these well. Through selling, you become more perceptive to things such as body language. You become a better listener, and you learn how to ask the right questions.

3. You learn important soft skills.

The sales process can often be a long, tedious one, involving a lot of back and forth between you and the prospective buyer. As you deal with different types of people, you will develop necessary soft skills to succeed in closing a sale. These include communication, presentation, persuasion, negotiation, and decision-making skills.

4. If you can sell something, you can sell anything.

The learnings you gain from working in sales is applicable in any industry. The abovementioned soft skills you learn can be used in to sell any product or service. Therefore, this means that it will not at all be a problem if you, for example, sell pharmaceuticals, and you decide to shift industry and sell houses instead. Once you know how to sell, you can sell absolutely anything under the sun to anyone.

5. You can start out with a sideline job for supplemental income.

If you are not ready yet to devote your entire time to selling, you can always try it out as a sideline job first. The best thing about most sales jobs is that you are in control of your own time, and that the rewards you reap is proportionate to the amount of work you put in. Practice and practice until sales talk feels not only comfortable to you but natural.

6. You can pitch ideas and get support.

Whether in your professional or personal life, you will have to use selling skills to propose ideas to other people, usually people of a higher authority who could support you in getting your proposal approved. This could be a proposal for financial backing to support your passion project or cause, or a proposal for a salary raise, or a proposal to upgrade your mobile data plan.

7. You can build your own business.

If you're thinking of starting your own business, selling abilities are essential. Even from the beginning, you need to be able to sell the concept of your business to potential investors, and then sell your product or service to the target market. No matter how great your concept, it doesn't matter if no one buys what you're offering; a business thrives through sales.

8. You can get rich.

Once you have mastered the art of selling, the likelihood of you earning a lot of money and getting rich is high. Excellent selling skills can open up many opportunities for you: significant commissions, corporate career promotion, lucrative business partnerships and deals, etc. If you look at most wealthy people, the secret to their success and how to get rich is usually taking a great idea and selling it really, really well.

9. You build connections with others.

Selling isn't always about money. Through your interactions with different kinds of people from different walks of life, you will be able to build invaluable and long-lasting connections. You will also have the opportunity to learn and exchange ideas and opinions with others, thus helping you to be a better-rounded person.

10. You need to know how to sell to survive.

Grant Cardone said that he got into sales so that he could survive. It's not all just about making money. You need to know how to sell in your everyday life, so that you can get what you want. When you ask someone for a loan, you need to sell to that person the benefits they will get out of giving you a loan. When you apply for a job, you need to sell to the interviewer your skills and convince him or her that you are the perfect candidate for the job. When you are on a date, you need to sell your personality to your date so that you can get a shot at a second date. You need to sell for survival, and you need to sell well to win at life.

The most essential thing to remember is: sales skills are not something you're born with; they are learned. Learning requires constant studying and practice. While the selling experience is always on a case-to-case basis, you can learn to sell and other important tips and tricks that are generally applicable to most people.

Bottom line is: you really need a strong commitment to learning in order to develop your sales skills and become not only a successful salesperson but a successful business person and entrepreneur.

Skill 5

<u>Being a Leader in your Field of Entrepreneurship</u>

Entrepreneurs are leaders in their own right. However, leadership is not only about titles. Leadership means guiding people towards the common goal and it will not be easy when people do not believe in you. To earn someone's trust takes a lot of effort, sacrifice, motivation, time and convincing power. Unfortunately, it only takes one big mistake to destroy that.

Good leaders have good followers. People listen to the person they trust and they obey their leader. If the people do not respect you, no matter what you do or what you say to them, they will not follow you. As an entrepreneur, you need to realize that the company does not revolve around you. The company revolves around the employees and your customers. Your role is to guide your employees towards the achievement of both personal and business goals.

5 Essential Characteristics of a Good Leader:

1. A leader should be credible:
   Credibility is one of the most important traits that leaders have to possess. If you want people to patronize your company and the products and services you provide, you need to maintain a good reputation. Leaders need to be credible to effectively communicate with their subordinates. In order to be credible, a leader should do what he says. Breaking promises and company's rules and regulations will merit distrust and will break people's loyalty not only to him as a leader but to the company in general.

2. A leader should be an expert in his own field:
   Being an expert does not mean you need to be all-knowing. Being an expert in the field means being able to see things that are not going well for the company and finding solutions to solve such problems. An expert knows what he is doing. In order for people to follow you, they need to know that you know what you are doing.

3. A leader is a visionary:
   Bill Gates, the richest man in the world and the owner of Microsoft - one of the most stable companies in the world started with a vision. He knew from the very beginning that even if the technology is not so advanced in the late 70's, the potential for a computer and software to

be a big business in the future is very high. He took the first radical step and now his business has earned him billions and billions of dollars in profit.

4. A leader is not afraid to take the risk:

Every good leader knows that risks are part of the game. They are not afraid to take drastic measures if needed. They are brave enough to try something new and if they fail, they are able to start again. Calculating the risks and preparing for the worst case scenario is one essential characteristic of a good leader and a successful entrepreneur. Warren Buffet and other investors always take the risk but they always manage to succeed.

5. A good leader is a good follower:

You cannot lead where you do not follow. Good leaders lead by examples and for that, they need to be good followers too. If you want your employees to come early, you need to be in your office early as well. If you want your employees to work harder, you need to work hard yourself. If you lead by example, it will not be difficult for you to make people listen. They will just follow you without you telling them to.

6

The Startup Business

Getting out of the rat race and gaining financial stability only has one solution – that is, to start your own business. However, this solution is not a path that everyone can walk on. This is because not all people are able to take the first step and establish their own business – it may be due to lack of funds or lack of knowledge on how to establish a startup business.

This chapter aims to give information about how anyone can properly establish their startup business. Aside from the basics of this concept, it will also discuss the important elements that will make it successful.

What you need to know about a startup business

Establishing your own business is one of the proven ways to bring financial stability to any person. However, not all people know how to set up their startup business as a way to achieve this goal.

This chapter will aim to discuss what this concept is about along with the basics surrounding it.

What is a startup business?

Whether you call it startup business, Startup Company, or startup alone, all of these terms only have one meaning. This concept refers to any business establishment that is still on its initial phase of operation. Startups aim to discover niches or fields in the market that can give profit to its originators.

What makes it different?

Although all businesses go through the initial phase of operation and always engage in researching the market, startups are still different from the usual form of (or non-startup) business.

The following points explain how these two are different:

Startup businesses can be temporary –

Unlike non-startup businesses, a startup could only be temporary. Think of it as a "hit and miss" activity, where the startup's originator presents an idea that may become an important product or service in the market when developed. If it goes well and somebody invests on the idea so that its end result can be reached, then they will gain funds and possible good profit from it should they wish to sell it (more of this on the succeeding chapters); otherwise, they abandon the business idea and will think of another concept for a startup business (after all, only a small amount of money was lost since it's still on the initial phase). On the other hand, non-startup businesses rely on the results of feasibility studies to see if their idea will bring them good sales before it is to be established.

Startup businesses rely on investors and outside financers –

One explanation as to why startups are temporary is that the funds needed for its operation depends on how many people will invest or how much will be invested for the development of the product or service. This is because most startup businesses require a large amount of capital before it can proceed with the succeeding phases of a business (mass production of the product or finding people who are capable of providing the service). Non-startup businesses, on the other hand, rely on the owner's funds (personally or through loans) to proceed with its operations.

Some of the systems that can be seen in an organization are absent in a startup business –

Unlike full-fledged business organizations, some startup types has a loose system. This is due to the fact that the latter only maintains a small team whose focus is on the development of the product or service – this is done so that the business concept can be pitched perfectly and, in turn, gains the attention of potential investors. Thus, there is no need to develop a detailed manual regarding rules and regulations or even develop of a good organizational structure for startup businesses. Only when the startup gains investments and is developed into an actual business organization that they should think of developing these systems.

Benefits of a startup business

Establishing a startup business does have its benefits, as explained on the following points:

There is low risk on your money –

A startup is something that you can engage in if you have the idea or concept but do not have the money to start it alone. Startups rely on presentations to gain investors; since you only maintain a few people to work for you during the development of the business idea or presentation, your limited budget will still suffice even if the concept did not go well.

It can be continued as a large organization –

Once you have enticed an investor to provide the budget that you need for the development of your business idea, you can continue the startup into a large organization. This is especially true if the concept that you have introduced is something that you are also interested with. Since it is your idea in the first place, it is assumed that you know how to make the business more marketable to consumers and be able to solve any problem that you might encounter.

You have the option to sell your idea and gain profit from it -

As mentioned on the previous section, most startup companies are temporary; not only due to its abandonment when it fails, but also when it has successfully attracted an investor. This is because as the one who conceived the idea, you have the right to sell your right/claim over the ownership of the business to the interested investor. By doing so, you get not only a good amount of money as payment for their "takeover" on your business but also the opportunity to work on another startup business or start an actual organization that is aligned to your interests.

Now that you have learned the basics on what a startup business is all about, the next section in this chapter will highlight the steps that you should take if you want the startup to become successful.

Learning what type of startup business are you starting

If you think startup businesses are same, you're wrong. This is because each business idea belongs to one of these business startup types.

This section will discuss what these types are. By knowing them, you get to know more about the appropriate system that you should use in order to increase your startup's chances of being successful.

As mentioned, knowing which type your startup business belongs can improve its chance for success. This is because in each startup type, there is an appropriate system that you should follow if you want it to end successfully. There may also be differences when it comes to key factors in your startup; some of these include the people that you should employ or work with (knowing who is fit for the job), the funds that it needs (what amount or equipment do you need), and other strategies that you need to use. By learning where does your startup belong, you will be able to change your system on these key areas and ensure success.

Your startup can fall in one of these six types:

Business startup for your lifestyle or passion –

Just as the name suggests, this startup type refers to businesses that you've started which is based on things that you have an interest. Typically, these types of businesses are small; after all, the aim of the owner is that they are doing something that they want while earning money from it. The earnings may not be very good, but it fulfills the owner's need. Those who engage in freelance work such as writing or making crafts are examples of startup businesses that fall under this type.

Buyable business startup –

There are also business concepts that are bound to be sold to investors in the future, hence the name "buyable". One guideline that you can use to see if your startup is under this type is if it takes too much time and effort for you to provide the product or service but doesn't give you an equitable profit given what you've spent on it. If you think that the product or service can do better when it comes to sales but you cannot reach the said target due to budget or equipment limitations and the like, you can look for a large company who can buy the startup and make it more successful in exchange for paying you a good amount of money. One example of this business startup is when you are able to develop a Web and mobile application. You may be able to make the app, but its maintenance can be bothersome (fixing bugs, changing interface, etc). This leads the developers to sell it to investors who can do the maintenance and give the right to sell it to their customers.

Small business startup –

This is the most common type of startup. If you want to establish a business with the goal of providing income for you and your family, your business startup is under this type. In this startup type, the funds mostly come from the owner and a few people (mostly family and friends). Another distinguishing feature of this startup type is that the owner doesn't have an interest (and does not make an effort) to sell the business to an investor. Unlike lifestyle startups however, this type earns enough profit. There may also be a need to hire people for this type of business. Small startups, however, do not maintain small for the rest of its existence. Should the owner wish to expand it, he or she can freely do so (although this is not the top priority of those who establish this kind of startup). Some examples of this startup business are grocery stores, consultancy firms, and home improvement companies.

Large business startups –

You also have the option to start a large business right from the beginning. Although it is mostly avoided by aspiring owners due to the very high risk that it carries, the product or service that you will be delivering somehow dictates the type where your startup will belong.

For example, car companies cannot be a small business startup; this is because for it to manufacture one car, it requires the work of a large team that will assemble the parts and operates the machines. One advantage that it has over its counterpart though, is that large businesses tend to produce a good amount of profit. It can also easily earn the trust of financial providers such as banks (this is because a business cannot become an organization if it doesn't have enough funds), making it easier for them to take out loans needed for their innovation and expansion.

Scalable startup business –

If you have the vision that your small business concept can be further improved and will become an indispensable product or service in the future, then your business is under this startup type. In a scalable business, the product/service should be constantly improved so that it becomes a good source of income. Once the business starts to gain popularity and has proven itself to be a good source of income, its owners can then sell it to interested parties for a very good price (due to its consistency in providing income). This type of business, however, requires more work compared to the previously mentioned types. This is because you will need to hire and maintain the best people for the job so that the product will be of high quality. It also involves risking funds; this is because once your team finds a scalable business niche, they will need more resources such as money to continue with its development and improvement. Some examples of businesses under this startup type are popular websites such as Google, Facebook, Skype, and Twitter.

Social startup business –

This is the least common of all startup types, primarily because most organizations under this type of business startup are non-profit. The goal of social entrepreneurs is to improve the world – not just make money. Different foundations that provide assistance to different kinds of people who need help such as out of school youth or malnourished children are examples of organizations that belong to this type of business. What makes some people engage in this startup (aside from the joy that helping others can give) is that they don't have to pay taxes due to them being non-profit. They can also earn money from pledges or charity work of people such as celebrities.

Now that you have learned about the types of business startups, you can now qualify which type your business concept belongs into. It is through knowing which startup type it belongs that you will be able to formulate the appropriate strategies that is suitable for each type.

Starting your startup business

If making the decision to start a business is hard, learning the proper way on how to start your startup business can be harder. Thus, you need to thoroughly prepare for several things before you start your startup.

Every business needs money to operate. Thus, for your startup to become successful, it needs to determine how much money is needed to start with the operation as well as where you can get it. The amount of money you need depends on the niche that you would want to penetrate. For the source of money, several sources are available.

Once you have the money that you need, make sure that you stick with your budget. As you are establishing a startup business, there is little assurance that it will return the money that you invested in it or it will even yield any profit at all. Thus, before you start, you need to learn how to control your spending. Stick with providing a budget for the essentials. This will help you prepare for emergency situations that may need financing.

Unless you will be working alone in your business, you also need to hire competent and trustworthy team members/employees and business partner. The people who surround you and will help you in operating or managing your business obviously will have an influence on the outcome of your startup. Make sure that whoever it is that you will hire can provide the quality of work that you expect from them.

Hone your social skills

Startup businesses can become more successful if those who manage it can easily interact with people. This will help them to find investors and other networks, as well as entice customers to try out their product or service. Inside the business, your good social skills will translate to better output from your team if you can socialize with them professionally and informally.

Now that you know what is needed to start your business, we will now discuss what you shouldn't be doing if you want your business to flourish.

Enumerating the don'ts in a startup business

It was mentioned earlier that startups carry lower risks, especially those that did not start as a large company. However, it doesn't mean that you can't make your startup fail in itself or that you can be complacent in running the business. After all, who wants to see their efforts wasted?

We will now look at the common mistakes that startup businessmen should avoid. By doing so, they become closer to their goal of making the startup successful.

-Keeping your "big idea" a secret

The first mistake that can make your startup fail is that if you always guard your "business concept" and refuse to share it with others.

Most startup owners are afraid that their "big idea" is all they have – and if somebody knew of it as well, they might act on it first and "steal" their chance from them. Business experts, however, encourage owners to be open in sharing their "big idea" due to the following reasons:

Business is not about ideas; rather, it's about execution – an idea in itself does not make it a business. As long as nobody is acting to turn the idea into an actual product or service, then it can never be considered as a business. Another point that you have to consider is that even if another person will "steal your big idea", the manner on how it will be implemented will be different. Thus, even if another person knows about your business concept, it doesn't guarantee that the method of implementation will bring it success.

Nobody can help you if the idea is closely guarded – if you don't want to divulge even the basic details in your business concept, even business experts cannot help you. It will be difficult for them to give you specific advises or insights if you are not willing to share the details in your business. It would be like telling your doctor that you're experiencing pain but not telling which area in your body is it coming from.

-Loss of Focus

Although a startup can become successful if its owner will always think of new ideas, there will come a time when you need to become intensely focused. Oftentimes, a startup owner has too many ideas that they tend to become lost as to what should they work on or where should they start. This can become disastrous when it comes to implementation.

It is advised that for an aspiring owner to turn his startup into a successful business, they need to maintain focused. Ideas are good and generate innovation; however, if you don't know the areas that you should focus, you will surely stir confusion to your team and ultimately lead it to failure. Know which systems work and stick on it. Or better yet, you can focus on improving this already useful practice rather than think of another idea that may not be as successful as the first. By doing so, you only get to improve or implement the practices that are giving you good results.

-Connecting on investors, not investees

Another common mistake made by startup business owners is that they are more concerned with getting connected with investors. Although this is exactly what they need to gain the capital for their business, there is an easier way to do it. This is to connect with the people that the investors have granted funds before and became successful. Aside from being an easier method of getting introduced to the investor, it also increases the chances that the investor will actually invest in your startup.

The following points will further explain why you need to start building connections with the investee:

The investees will serve as your way to the investor – before these investees became popular and successful, they also experienced the same problem that you're experiencing now (that is, they are also pursuing for people who can invest on them). Since they know what you are experiencing, they may be compelled to help another aspirant who wants to succeed in their business. As long as the product or service that you will be presenting is repeatable and will provide a steady source of income, the investees will be more than happy to "refer" you to their investors. With this, you are able to connect with both the investee and the investor.

You get to learn more from someone who started with a startup – aside from being connected with the investor, you also get to learn something from the investee. This is especially true if you are able to meet an investee that is in the same or similar niche where you want to establish your business.

-Taking too long to launch the business

Most startup owners think that for the business to become truly successful, everything should be perfect from day 1. Although it is true that success depends on the quality of product or service that you deliver, what's most important in a startup business is that it should be able to penetrate the target market as early as possible. As long as the end product is of good quality, the startup will most likely get the attention of customers. They may even want to be updated as to the improvements that you will implement in your business so that they can be provided with a better product/service. Business experts suggest that once you've penetrated the market, it will be easier for you to plan for improvements, get investors, and expand.

-Trying to please everyone

If you want your startup to become successful, you need to realize early that you can never please everyone – customers and your team/employees alike. This is because if you spend too much time just to turn skeptics into supporters or loyal customers of your company, you will be wasting an important resource that could have been spent on improving your relationship with people who already believe in your business, are willing to invest, and will buy your product even without too much persuasion or marketing. Spend your time with people who will lift your business and help it become successful – not on people that you need to woo first in order to get their approval.

Now that you know the common mistakes that may be hindering your startup's success, it's time to do something to correct these practices. By doing so, your startup will be one step closer to being more successful.

Financing options for startup businesses

All types of business, even the smallest ones, need capital in order to start with its operations. In a startup business, it is common practice that the business owner finds an investor who can provide the budget that they need. The term investor, however, is relative. This is because there are many financing options available to anyone who wants to establish their startup.

5 Common Financing Options

Before the person starts seeking for outside help, they should at least try to generate money on their own using the concept of sweat equity.

In sweat equity, you make use of unpaid services as well as labor so that your startup can build its value. These "unpaid services and labor", of course, refers to using your own skills and time – with the business' eventual success as your salary. This lets you save your precious money on other things.

Working for free, though, has its advantages. Since you do not need to look for someone who will work for you, the control as to everything related to the product or service is on you. One business that started with this financing option is Facebook (Mark Zuckerberg and his friends started the site in a Harvard dormitory).

-Family and friends

The first network of people that any businessman has is their family members and circle of friends. Thus, it is also practical that before they start looking for other investors, they should first seek the help of these people.

Asking your family and friends for money to fund your startup business is mostly positive, as they are people who will most likely support you unconditionally. As long as you are able to present proof that your startup is doing well and that it will produce a good amount of profit, they will rarely say no to your request.

One drawback of this option, however, is you need to properly document your dealings with them and clarify the terms of the loan. Since they are closely related to you and are lending you money, they might assume that they are also owners in your startup business.

-Using your savings

If you strongly believe that your startup can be a good source of profit once it was financed, owners can also opt to risk their own money so that the business will be launched as soon as possible. Not only are you in total control of the business (since the concept and the money is yours), you are also careful when it comes to the expenses, making sure that you are only spending on essentials. As long as you know how to keep records and balance your income and expenses, this option can be utilized.

-Venture capital

Another financing option is to look for venture capital firms. These firms operate by providing a large amount of money to be used as capital for your startup business. However, these firms will only take interest in your business if your presentation shows that its development will ensure a high return rate for the investment. They will also invest if your business has a marketable product or service that can generate continuous profit. This is a good financing option for those who are planning to build a large startup business.

Should your business be funded by a VC firm, you also get guidance from business and management experts so that the investment will be maximized and generate a huge profit. One disadvantage of this method, however, is that the firm will be eyeing for a position in the board of directors. This is to closely monitor where the money is going and influence the decisions of other board members as to which projects are most profitable.

-Acquisitions and mergers

If your startup is a buyable or scalable business (see Chapter 2), being acquired or merged by another company will be the source of your money. This is because an acquisition or merger refers to the process in which a large company will be buying or will team up with a small company whose product or service is similar to theirs and can generate a good source of income in itself. One business that experienced this financial method is Instagram.

By learning about the different financing options that you can use to fund your startup business, you can choose accordingly as to which of the above mentioned methods is best for your startup.

Conclusion

Establishing a startup business is not a walk in the park. It involves knowing the basics such as the do's and don'ts, the type of your startup business, and the different financial options that you can utilize to gain funds for the business.

7

Online Entrepreneurship

Why Now Is a Good Time to Be an Online Entrepreneur

With the rise in the number of internet users, the world-wide web has become a new arena for entrepreneurs and aspiring businessmen. The field of entrepreneurship has taken a whole new level by entering the online world.

Online entrepreneurs have begun to emerge, showing people how to get rich in a different way. To keep up with the times and remain competitive, traditional, long-term businesses also entered the scene to make money online.

Having an online business does not only help you earn more money, but could also help you grow as an entrepreneur. Here, we have laid out a number of reasons why you should become an online entrepreneur now, and how you can get rich by starting an online business.

It is less expensive

Starting an online business is less expensive, because it requires a low start-up cost. You do not need to spend your money to buy a physical lot for your business, or build an office that would require you to spend on materials you will need. You also do not need to spend so much on water and electricity bills that you would normally have to include in your budget when owning a physical business, because everything is done online. You can pay less to get a domain name and hosting for your site.

It is easier to start

Building your own business online is easier because you do not need to go through the hassle of going to the site where your establishment is being constructed, and you do not need to worry about looking for a good location that would provide you with an excellent market. All you have to do is create your own account in online website shops, or create your own site and slowly let your business grow by getting more viewers and having ads posted in your site.

It is less risky

The reality is that not everyone who starts a business would end up successful, which is why most people would not risk spending too much on creating a business that would not ensure profits. Creating an online business is less risky, because in case of a major crash in your business, it is easier to get back on your feet since you are not faced with a ton of financial problems like paying for loans and wasted money on materials.

It is easier to manage

Since most of the work you will be doing is done through the internet and on your laptop, online businesses are easier to manage and track. With all the new features and benefits provided by hosting sites, constructing your online business can be done with ease.

You do not have to worry about traffic

One of the perks of having an online business is that you do not have to go out of your house and go through congested cars in order to get to your office. Being an online entrepreneur allows you to work in the comfort of your own home, wearing your favorite comfortable pajamas while drinking a cup of coffee or tea.

Flexible working schedule

Working online gives you a more flexible working schedule, allowing you to work for a few days in a week. When you need to work or monitor your business, all you have to do is open your laptop and get to your task.

You can work anywhere in the world

Imagine going out on vacation with your family when you realize that you forgot to do some unfinished tasks in your business at home. Having an online business would prevent you from having this problem, since you can access your work even when you are on vacation in case of an emergency.

You can provide more efficient work

An online business would help you produce more efficient results, since you get to work on your desired time in your intended number of hours. Also, most people who build online businesses usually build something out of their passion, and when you are doing what you love, you produce better results.

You control your work

Being a new online entrepreneur would usually mean that you start by personally managing all the parts of your business. You become your own boss, and all the work that you've done is credited to no one else but you – your work is truly your own. You build your business the way you want it to be, and you are free to use your creativity when creating your logo, site, name, and so much more.

You help provide jobs

Once your online business has grown and becomes difficult to manage alone, you begin to hire people to help you track and control your business activities. You do not only earn by doing what you love in the comfort of your own home, but you also help the economy by providing jobs.

You have more time to do other things

Flexible working schedules and being your own boss allows you to have more time for yourself. You now have the chance to spend more time with your kids, take some baking lessons, do yoga, walk your dog, go on vacation, and enjoy other leisure activities.

There is a wide range of opportunities

The online world provides new businesses with a ton of opportunities, in order to cater to the different needs of different types of entrepreneurs and consumers. Social media platforms provide new online entrepreneurs with an opportunity to share their newly started businesses in order to increase their market and strengthen their brand. Aside from this, sites have a way of gathering data, in order to determine what your audience are interested in and what they want to buy.

You can earn unlimited income

Unlike working on regular jobs, getting an online business does not require you to work a number of hours in order to earn a certain amount of money. Your productivity in fewer hours is more important than working long hours and producing less. You can engage in income generating and marketing activities in order to earn even when you are asleep. When your business becomes stronger and more reliable, companies would want to invest in your site by promoting their brands in your website, helping you earn 24/7, 365 days a year.

It makes you more productive on the internet

Running an online business, no matter how small, is extremely helpful, especially for those who spend a lot of time on the world-wide web. Having an online business makes you more productive online, instead of just wasting your time playing games or procrastinating.

You can still keep your day job

The good thing about being an online entrepreneur is that you could juggle day tasks while still earning passively online. You do not need to quit your day job once you've started your online business, but most of the time, when businesses grow, online entrepreneurs go hands-on.

You can lower your household and childcare expenses

Since you now spend more time at home, you can cut down on your childcare expenses and watch your kids instead – send them to school, help them with their homework, and spend more time with them. You can also cut down on household expenses by doing some of the housework yourself.

It is easier to build networks

With the abundance of social media users and web surfers, it is much easier for you to build your network for online businesses compared to physical ones.

There's always room for growth

If you are afraid that you are too late to start your online business, you must remember that the online world is still growing, and a lot of different opportunities are in store for various types of entrepreneurs. There will always be newer ways to increase your earning potential; all you have to do is be updated with the latest trends and features. Online businesses will always have room to grow as entrepreneurs explore their interests and establish better things to sell to their audience.

You can reach out to people

Online entrepreneurs have the ability to reach out to people from around the globe and influence them to support their business, depending on how efficient their marketing strategies are. Having an online business could also be an opportunity for you to share your advocacy to the world, and let people participate in your different activities. You get to strengthen your brand and increase your market while promoting something good.

It helps you become more disciplined

Having flexible working schedules and not having to get out of the house to work sounds great, but it could also breed laziness. This is why online entrepreneurs need to learn to be disciplined, in order to ensure that their businesses would flourish. It encourages you to grow as a person and become more responsible and mature.

With a growing access to audiences from around the world, low costs, and so much more, building an online business would be a great move. It's time for you to take the challenge and present your ideas to the world.

How to Get Rich Online

Tired of the cyclical routine in the corporate set-up? Need extra source of income? Got lots of time to kill at home? Thanks to the innovative platforms available on the internet, earning extra income online had become a widely prevalent practice these days.

With just a handy gadget, an internet connection and extra time, anyone can earn extra cash through numerous ways online. From selling, marketing, writing and even trading, versatile opportunities online are available, that would surely help in footing the bills.

Many people choose a home-based online job mainly due to the flexible time it provides and assistance in financial security. It allows for a work-life balance that most 9-5PM desk jobs do not provide.

Instead of wasting time watching videos, or mindlessly browsing through your Facebook News Feed here are ten easy ways to keep the cash flowing, through online opportunities:

(1) YouTube

According to site ranking group Alexa, You Tube is one of the most visited all across the globe. Hence, a lot of so called professional YouTubers have already found a promising source of living through their own channel in the video streaming site. The trick is simple – create a channel, earn followers, get promising hits and get paid for every single ad viewed by the audience from your videos.

Some of the most popular YouTubers like Pewdiepie, Markiplier and Jacksepticeye cater to the younger audience, mainly discussing online games, RPGs and the likes. What makes them effective is their delivery of video blogging that will keep the audience engaged.

The secret? Create an inviting title, make your thumbnail attention grabbing and spark curiosity from your potential viewers.

(2) Blogging

You probably had already come across artsy photos on Instagram, where each and every single clothing is worn in the photo is tagged. In this digital age, blogging has officially become an accepted way of living. A lot of personalities often tagged as **'social media influencers'**, are earning income through blogging. This can either be for travel lifestyle, fashion, food or even beauty. Bloggers write on what the audience would want to read, and they get paid for it.

When you look at your blog, try asking yourself, Could I be making money from this? Of course you can! You've put the hard work and heart into your words; it is time to reap the rewards. While you may feel that throwing some Ads onto your website may be the answer, I'm are here to open your eyes to a whole new world. Luckily, there are several tricks to get you started whether you are a blogging beginner or an expert on the internet.

I got you covered!

The Goal

In the case that you are just getting your blog started, it is very important to monetize your blog. The key goal for your blog is to get a regular traffic stream. There are several ways to get the visitors and keep them coming back for more. You should keep in mind that each blog is different. What one blog may receive in visitors, may be drastically different from your visitors.

You will want to make sure you find a popular niche. People are coming to your blog for one reason, and one reason only. Your readers have questions! Your job is to make sure your blog has the answers. Once you build trust from your readers, it is time for target practice. For your readers, that is!

As you build your blog, be sure to always keep your audience in mind. If your blog is all about you, you may as well just keep a journal. Your blog should include aspects that will be important to your readers. Your audience will each have a specific need, think of the different ways you can offer answers to all of their problems. This is one reason we suggest sticking with one niche. When you try to offer too much, it will become difficult for people to find the answers they are looking for. With a specific niche, it will make monetizing much easier for you. We believe that there is a method for everyone. Check out just some of your options below!

Top Monetizing Methods

Method # 1: Affiliate Sales

If this seems intimidating, don't let it be! In basic terms, you will be getting paid by a recommended product. All you will need to do is link either an online service or a specific product to your blog. When you are getting more and more visitors, there is a higher chance of a reader clicking on the link to purchase something. When this happens, you will get a portion of the sale. See? It is super simple! If you are looking for a quick and simple affiliate sale, check out Amazon. All you do is place a link to the Amazon product, and you are ready to go!

Method # 2: Sell Yourself

Ok, not really. That is illegal. But, you can sell your incredible skills! You are worth more than you could ever imagine. With your blog, you can show your skills off even further and prove yourself to your audience. When you showcase your graphic design skills, coding skills, or even writing skills, it is a fantastic way to make money. When people see your skills live in action, they would be more likely to turn to you for advice. One way to make some extra cash is to offer your talents through coaching and e-courses. You will be surprised how many people will follow you to learn skills such as application designing, or anything that you have to offer!

Method # 3: Sell Products

While some people use a blog to write, others use their blog to sell! When you do it the right way, selling product can be one of the best ways to monetize your blog! While we have discussed selling other people's products, why not sell your own? Of course, you should realize that this is going to take some extra work, but you get what you work for! When you think about it, you will get to keep all of the profit! There are options out there if you don't feel selling a product is up your ally.

First, you could sell a physical product. Remember that your audience is on your blog searching for answers. When you look at your niche, is there a product in the realm to make their lives easier? Is there something that could benefit your life? Most of the time, the answer is absolutely! We live in an instant reward society; there is always room for improvement.

If a physical product isn't for you, try a digital product! We are in a digital age; the options are endless! To start, we suggest writing an eBook. Not much of a writer? There is a ghostwriter for that! If you are more technologically knowledgeable, try offering an application for your readers. In the end, you just want to be sure that everything you sell if affordable. The more you sell, the more you will make between the blog and the product!

Method # 4: Membership

When you look at your blog, you must ask yourself if you have everything you need to offer? When you offer a membership, you will want to make sure your content is enticing enough. The key is to get them hooked enough, that they will pay for a premium service. If you look at Netflix and Spotify, they do the same thing. They offer a free monthly trial, get you addicted to the media, and then you will pay for the premium membership to make it convenient for you. In your case, you will want to give your readers a taste and make them pay for more.

Another way to do this for a blog is to have what is known as "gated content." With this method, your reader will need a subscription to be able to read everything they want on your blog. With this, you will want to be careful. For small blogs, people would probably just find their answers somewhere else. Instead of a subscription, you can offer detailed guides for a small price. This way, you are offering great advice on your blog, but even better advice for a small fee.

Method # 5: Classic Ads

This is the most common way to make money from your blog. We saved this for last as we wanted to show you that there are other ways to make money. While there is a debate on whether or not advertisements work, they will make you money. The key is having a lot of traffic. If your blog isn't super popular, you should try including other revenue sources. One of the most popular options is to use Google AdSense. As soon as you sign up, you will begin to see adverts showing up on your blog. If you are a beginner, this is a fantastic way to dip your toes into making money. As you become more popular, you can graduate to private advertisements and make even more money!

All About the Benefits

At the end of the day, who wouldn't want to make extra money? You are putting the work into it; you might as well get even more out of your effort. On top of making money, you will be making money doing what you love. (Hopefully) As you work harder, remember that you will want to remain dedicated to your blog. Many people have their hearts in the right place, but blogging isn't always easy. On the days that you feel like there is nothing to write about, remind yourself why you are running a blog in the first place. If you truly love the niche, there is always something to write about and to learn. Remind yourself that your people need you. The harder you work to get an audience, the more money you will make. It is all about dedication. Remind yourself that you can do it!

But how does that work exactly?

Blogging, as one of the most effective ways on how to become rich online, mainly works through ad placements on a blogger's site, sponsored content, paid reviews and partnerships. The higher the audience, the higher would be the pay. This is typically measured through analytics such as pay per click, pay per view and outbound clicks. Hence, the more efficient you are in selling the product to your readers, the more likely you would get paid higher.

(3) Freelance Writing

Love writing, but not fit to publish your own manuscript? Why not try freelance writing? The ultimate weapon on online sites and pages are their content – these must always be fresh, updated and informative. Freelance writers are employed to keep these pages relevant, up-to-date and ahead in SERPs, or search engine results page. Being a freelance writer means having the liberty to work anytime, anywhere and at your preferred pace. All you have to do is to sell the brand in a natural sounding manner, incorporate the keywords and ensure readability of your articles.

(4)Selling products

Of course, the internet has also become a great avenue for selling. E-commerce will always be an efficient and convenient way to earn extra income online because it drops all overhead costs involved in putting up a physical store.

This could also be a good way to ignite your business concept. Have a product in mind like clothing, food or even services? The internet can be a good place to test the waters without having to shell out too much capital funds. Becoming an entrepreneur and being able to track your sale easily are among the perks of being an online seller.

Apart from that, the marketing efforts can be easily done through social media sites which are usually free of charge.

(5) Home based social media manager

Always on Facebook? Well, time to turn that Facebook hours into something productive by being a community manager!

Some companies choose to outsource their online marketing activities which are typically done by agencies. These agencies place a professional fee for representing the brand online. However, some businesses – typically the start-ups, choose to hire an individual to do the basic social media community engagement tasks. Usual tasks of an admin of a certain Facebook, Twitter or Instagram page of a brand include providing real-time responses to each query and re-posting content. The key is to boost the reach of the page, cater to its customers, and keep the site updated.

(6) Selling your own video

Love video filming? Why don't you turn that hobby into a money making activity! Selling videos online have become a very common source of income opportunity in the internet. Similar to stock images, videos can also be bought by companies or brands for their own use. Some popular sites to bid out your videos include VHX, Gumroad, Chill, Tinypass, Pivotshare, Redux and of course, YouTube.

(7) Self-Publishing on Amazon

Have you always wanted to be a writer? Getting noticed by publishing houses can be quite a challenge, especially given the tough competition these days. With that, Amazon is here to the rescue! You may now earn money through self-publishing. This is one of the online opportunities that have sparked hope to a lot of writers. For instance, hit series writer EL James sold over 250 thousand copies of her Fifty Shades novels before she became professionally published.

KDP Amazon, is where you can have your book published. Simply prepare a manuscript, create a KDP account, select the box that you intend to be both Kindle and paperback, choose a cover and finally, upload your manuscript. Within a few days, people may start buying your book on Amazon.

Some people choose self-publishing over traditional publishing not merely because of money, but also due to foreign rights and other packages that you receive if all rights and trademark relating to your work is on your hands.

Amazon is one of the biggest online retailers that you are going to find. If you are an author, publishing on Amazon can end up bringing you a lot of money. But, how are you going to be able to make money on Amazon? In this section, we are going to look at how you can make money off your ebooks on Amazon.

Taking advantage of the Kindle platform that Amazon has to offer is going to be one of the best decisions that you are going to make when it comes to publishing books online because it is fairly simple to follow the layout and get your book out across the world for everyone to read. It does not matter if you are publishing for the first time or for the hundredth time because with Amazon, it does not matter. You are going to be able to establish yourself and gather a good following of people by using Amazon to publish.

Whenever you are publishing on Amazon, you are going to want to take advantage of Kindle Direct Publishing or KDP because this is going to get your book published faster than going the traditional Amazon publishing route. Not only that, but you are going to get a larger percentage of sales by using KDP.

You can also make it to where your book is only available for free on KDP. In doing this, you are going to be promoting your fans to tell their friends about your book. Not every Amazon book buyer has KDP so there are going to be people who buy your book the traditional way which means that they are going to be paying the amount that you are wanting for your book. Of course, this is going to depend on the quality of your work as well too.

The first thing that you are going to want to do is find the proper category for your writing. Every category of writing goes through its phases of being popular or not. You do not have to change every time that your category goes through a down phase. However, it is going to be more beneficial to you if you find a category that is going to not only be profitable but is also not going to have much competition. The less competition that you have to beat out, the easier it is going to be for the customer to come to you and buy your book. With that being said, you need to keep in mind that you should be knowledgeable on the category that you are writing about. Do not just write something because there is less competition and you think you can make money in that category.

Should you still be trying to find what you are wanting to write about, you need to see if you are going to actually sell any books if you were to write in that category. There are some things that are not going to do well if they are sold online because people are not interested in that topic. Or, if they are, there is not a very wide audience. You are going to have to be careful with what you decide to write. For example, if you are writing a fiction book about a brother and sister going to the park, you are going to have a small audience of people who are going to be interested and buy your book, but it is not going to last very long.

The title and cover are what sells the book. If your title is not eye-catching, and your cover does not give some indication of the book, then you are not going to sell books. Think of it in terms of what you would want to see on the cover of a book. Would you buy a book on how to fix a car, but has a unicorn on the cover? Chances are that you won't. In fact, you would probably be thinking what on earth does a unicorn have to do with fixing a car!

Once you have decided what it is that you are going to write, you are going to want to write your book. If you do not want to write your book yourself, then you can always hire someone else to do it for you. There are plenty of ghostwriter companies out there that are going to be willing to write your book for a small fee. When you are writing your book, think about the length. The length is going to determine what it is that you are going to price your book at. Many books are not going to be hard to write and can usually be written inside of a week depending on the topic.

Publishing. As we mentioned before, publishing with Amazon is not hard. In fact, they walk you through the steps on how you will publish your book. It is not going to be published right away because Amazon goes over it before it is published. The most important things you will need to have before your book is published is the book's title, cover, description. And, of course, the book itself. When you are choosing your royalties, you are going to see that you can either get 35% or 70% of the profits. Amazon will determine which one you are going to get based on what you are going to price your book at. You will also need to determine if you want your book to be available throughout the entire world or in certain parts of the world.

One thing that makes or breaks a book is the reviews that it gets. You will have noticed that with Amazon, there are two different types of reviews, the ones that you are going to want to get more of are the verified reviews because these are the ones that mean that your book was bought by an Amazon customer. The more reviews you get and the better the reviews are, the higher you are going to be on the Amazon ranking system. The higher that you are, the more likely it is that your book is going to be found by Amazon customers when they do their searches.

Amazon offers promotions where your book will be offered for a cheaper price or is put at the top of searches for a short period of time. It is going to be up to you as to how you take advantage of Amazon's promotion's that they offer. If you do not want to take advantage of them, you do not have to. You can always do your own promotion and this is going to help push people towards your book as well. Some of the things that Amazon offers are

KDP: this is going to be where you can put your book up for free as well as be able to put your book on the countdown deals. The bad thing about KDP Select is that your book cannot be published anywhere else on the web while it is enrolled in this program.

Countdown deals: your book can go up for a discounted price as we have discussed. So, if your book is $3.00 and you want to give your readers a discount but not a permanent one, you are going to be able to use countdown deals to discount your book for as long as you want it discounted before it goes back to your normal price.

Publishing on Amazon is a great way that you can make money with your ebook.

In the end, write whatever you want to write because you are going to make money off of it as long as your writing quality is good and you market your book properly.

(8) Affiliate Marketing

You have probably come across someone who's been trying to sell something and attempted recruiting you as part of their group? Affiliate marketing, a type of a multi-level marketing scheme, is also prevalent in the online world. The online version is much more convenient than the traditional one. It typically involves enrolling in an affiliate marketing group, selling the product through clicks, links and posts, and earning through a click per share basis. This is somewhat similar to blogging and internet marketing, except that this works under a specific system or group. Think of it this way – for every click translated into a sale, and for every additional recruit to the team, you get a commission straight to your pocket. How does that sound?

Here's How ClickBank Can Help You Earn More

ClickBank's affiliate marketing program is a good way to earn additional income. It's a preferred program by online marketers because it's not complicated to understand. It's an ideal source of passive income because you just need to follow the rules and the commissions will then come.

Before anything else, what is ClickBank?

What Is Clickbank?

Founded in San Diego, California, ClickBank is an affiliate marketing company handling physical and digital products. It's a website that consumers go to if they wish to buy items such as eBooks and various software programs.

What ClickBank does is to act as a middle man between content creators and affiliate marketers. It's in charge of calculating tax charges, checking payments and providing customer service duties.

ClickBank can benefit three groups of people:

The customers, by providing them the items that they need,
   the product creators who come up with the objects that solve the consumers' needs **and the affiliate marketers** also benefit by gaining commissions from the sales of the products to the consumers.

Today, ClickBank is one of the top affiliate networks and is a well-trusted Internet retailer. It assists in generating revenue for affiliate marketers and has reached 200 million customers worldwide.

A Good Marketing Strategy

Choosing ClickBank as an affiliate marketing partner is a good strategy as it can easily manage around 30,000 digital sales each day. It also has 6 million registered users who promote the site's digital programs.

As of 2011, ClickBank has been able to provide assistance to more than 600 countries and has managed to promote around 46,000 products.

How to make money online through ClickBank?

You can create your own product and use ClickBank to sell it, or
You can be a ClickBank affiliate. i.e. someone who sells products in ClickBank's behalf.

If you don't have a product to sell, then opt to be an affiliate instead and still make money. How? Promote the products on your site and lead the interested prospects back to ClickBank. Once the prospect completes the sale, then you get a commission from it.

Many affiliate marketers are satisfied with their venture with ClickBank. The company makes sure that the marketers are paid promptly and accurately. They are even provided with helpful analytics, enabling them to study their earnings, and get into partnerships to produce higher sales and get better commissions.

Making Money from Clickbank

How to make money online through Clickbank? Just follow these steps to get you started.

1- Choose the product you're going to sell.

It won't be easy to choose a product – after all, the company literally has thousands of them — but to make the task less difficult, pick out one that fits your site or your interests the most. Doing this will also make it easier for you to promote the product.

In choosing the product, there are different factors to consider:

Gravity — This refers to the number of affiliate marketers who are already promoting the product. If there are too many of you who are promoting the item, then it would be better choose a different item to advertise.

Dollar per Sale — How much will you make for each sale?
   Average Percent per Sale — How much commission will the vendor will be giving for every sale?

Take note of all these factors especially if you're an affiliate marketing beginner. All of these will contribute to successful promotions and excellent sales.

2-Promote your chosen product.

Being able to choose the product does not mean you're all done.
   After you've decided which product you'll be selling, you can now click on the 'Promote' button. After clicking the button, a URL link will pop up. Copy and save the link — this link is what you'll be using to promote the product.
   How will you promote the product? You can use the following tools:

- Your personal blog
- Free classified websites
- Social media sites e.g. Twitter and Facebook
- An article to promote the product
- YouTube videos

- Email and/or search engine marketing

Pick among those methods, find which ones work best for you and use that to endorse your preferred product.

3-Sell and earn from your product.

Now that you've picked out your product and your selling method, it's time to sell and make money using those tools.

Paste the link that you've copied earlier on your site or blog. Once your blog is published, anyone who visits your site and clicks your link will be routed to the product page where they can purchase it.

If the customer ends up buying your product, you'll receive your commission. This amount will be automatically credited to your account. The more products you sell, the more commissions you'll be receiving.

ClickBank will pay you each month once you've reached $100 in your account.

Making the Most of Clickbank

Want to boost your earnings? Try out these tips to help maximize the profits you'll be getting from ClickBank.

Choose a good product that fits your audience. No matter how good your product is, if the right people don't find out about it, then your efforts will be pointless.

Utilize tools to maximize your sales. There are software programs you can use to further improve your sales rates. There are also free tools that you can use if you want no additional charges – the tools allow you to see products with highest gravity rates, popularity, recurring income and other factors.

While it's true that the higher the gravity, the more people are earning, you should also remember that some newly released products have low gravity but are also potential hot sellers. Observe and study the product first to see how it will perform.

Aside from Facebook and Twitter, try out other sites to promote the product such as Pinterest and Instagram. A lot of people are using them, which can lead to more traffic for your site.

Those are just few of the tips you can try out to boost your earnings from ClickBank affiliate marketing. Soon, you'll discover other ways of adding more to your earnings.

Conclusion

Don't be afraid to try out ClickBank. A lot of people have proven its legitimacy in earning commissions from selling products. It's a good source of passive income because all you need is to set up your site, choose products, paste the link, and that's it.

All you need is to find out ways on how to boost your earnings. Once you do, it'll be a good source of proceeds to complement your income.
    Don't have an account yet? Visit their site and create your own ClickBank account. Creating an account is free of charge. Soon, you'll earn and receive the commissions from the products that you sell.

(9) Stock Market (Forex)

Apart from the open market which mostly involves equity, forex trading is also a platform where you can earn a lot of money. Foreign exchange, widely known as 'Forex' or 'FX', is the market driven exchange from one specified currency for another at an agreed price being bit through over-the-counter markets worldwide. You can earn money by buying your forex money at a low price, and correspondingly selling it once the market prices turn out higher. Forex is one of the most active markets with an average turnover of about US $5 trillion daily.

How to Make Money as a Forex Trader Online

In the rubble of today's financial crisis's, it is no secret that majority of us have spent countless hours pondering over how we can build a more stable financial foundation for ourselves now, as well as for our inevitable futures. There are many individuals who have spent endless time that we cannot get back glued to the Google search results, hoping for a miraculous answer on ways to make money in honest ways. Perhaps we are all spending too much time searching in the wrong places, and need to view ourselves in a more professional light when it comes how we make and spend our hard earned cash.

You either came across this article during one of your sleepless late-night desperate Google searches, or you are here because you have actually heard and want to hone your skills as an online trader. I know what you are thinking, "Trader?! Nope. Nu-uh. I am not smart enough, nor am I equipped with the green to be able to do such a thing." Well, I am here to tell you to rethink what you "know" about trading.

Yes, the world of trading, let alone virtual trading, can be so broad that it is nauseating. But, have you ever heard of Forex Trading? Well, in a nutshell, this is the umbrella where ALL global currencies trade. That makes for quite the umbrella, but bear with me! With its size comes the title of being the most liquid markets in the world. Forex trading is pretty similar to stock trading, but with one awesome exception. You can conduct Forex trades 24/7! This helps those that do this gain major exposure to international markets.

When it comes to anything in life that is among any complexity, it is vital to have a good understanding and vocabulary on the subject at hand. So, let's dumb Forex trading down and bit, and break it down for better understanding.

Forex is most abbreviated in the terms of "foreign exchange." Both investors and speculators trade within this market. For example, let's compare the good ol' U.S. dollar to a euro. Perhaps the U.S. dollar is foreseen to decline? More than likely in this type of situation a forex trader will sell dollars to purchase euros, for when the euro strengthens, the purchasing power to then buy dollars has increased. Which in turn means the trader can buy back MORE dollars than what they originally had to start out with, making a profit.

The secret to Forex Trading is initially all within the exchange. Exchange rates that is! The foreign exchange market itself is a marketplace that determines the values of different currencies. The existence of currency is more vital in conducting foreign business than any one person realizes. The livelihood behind forex marketing is the need to network! The size of Forex marketing makes other areas of commerce looks sizably smaller, with a traded value of $2,000 billion per DAY. And yes, that is in U.S. dollars. With all that green flying around to different places, you may be wondering how YOU can get in on just a tiny piece of this action! Well, you are in the right place.

If you are to be truly successful in the ways of Forex trading, you are going to need to have a few key know-how's and a couple tricks under your belt to really know what you are doing, especially when your own earnings are at stake. Next are some things to keep in mind from experts in Forex trading themselves!

Analyze Your Needs, Plan Goals and Stick to It!
To be able to receive any profit in the world of trading, you first must know the signs of recognizing markets. But, hold those horses! Before that step, you firstly have to get to know your true self. Understanding your needs can help you define your risk tolerance! Taking the time to ensure that your capital quotas and risk tolerance are in balance and not either excessive or lacking is an important step many people think through too quickly. Studying and analyzing your financial goals and dreams is just as engaging as taking a leap into the actual trading process.

Once you figure out what you initially WANT from trading, you can honestly define your goals and the timeframe you would like to meet those goals. Knowing how much time you can devote to trading is a big step into achieving the goals you want out of this venture. Having concise goals makes it easier to stick to trading, as well as ease in jumping ship if risks overshadow your profit too much for comfort.

Pick Account Type that Works for You

It is important that you choose an account package that as the ability to leverage ratios in accordance with your wants, needs and expectations of trading. This step can be a bit confusing, especially as a beginner. The general rule to follow is the lower the leverage, the better the bet. For beginners it is recommended that a period of studying and practicing how a certain account may leverage happens before really committing to an account type. This can be done by the utilization of a mini account. The rule of thumb: the lower the risk, the higher your chances. So it is smart to be conservative as a beginner in this field.

Bigger is Not Always Best

An ounce of wisdom in getting your feet wet with Forex trading is learning that small sums can get you farther than depositing large sums. Small sums equal lower leverages. This does not mean if you are feeling like living on the edge a bit not to do so, but as a beginner it can be wise to start small and see where it gets you. You may be surprised that your tinier investments may get your more profit than those that pump large sums of money into their accounts.

Act On Understanding

Forex trading is not the time to be acting upon things just because you believe you get the "gist" of them. The world of currency is deeply vast and wildly complicated. This is because of the very chaotic nature that markets tend to have. Even for those that are experienced, it is hard to master all the different kinds of financial activity that goes on in the corners of the planet. It is wise to start with the trading of currency you know well, such as your own country. Either that or stick to those trades that are most liquid.

"Success Is Never Permanent and Failure Is Never Fatal"

This quote should be lived by within all aspects of life, but especially in the world of Forex trading. It is important to know that you will fail, probably A LOT, before you really start to get the hang of how it works, and how it can initially work for you! Make sure you take physical or mental notes, studying both your successes and failures. You will start to grasp a deeper understanding from the very first dollar you invest into the circulations of the Forex. Keeping track of all your trading activities, along with hard work, will land you in a sweet spot, all thanks to the ways of Forex marketing!

8

Social Media Marketing For Online Businesses

Before the World Wide Web, businesses depended primarily on "word of mouth" marketing of their business by consumers. This as well as television and radio ads that most consumers tuned out as soon as they began airing, were the primary venues associated with marketing. Today social media outlets have allowed online businesses to get the word out more quickly and efficiently, and have also created a gateway for controlling the image businesses are presenting to the public.

It takes time and patience to build a strong presence for your online business but the perks of social media marketing can be invaluable. Business recognition and quality control are things that could break a marketing budget with traditional marketing techniques. Social media marketing gives you, the business owner, the control and power to drive your success in a more cost-effective manner while also allowing you to create and meet your time constraints.

Business Recognition

Everyone is using social media these days; it's not limited only to connecting with your family and friends. It's everywhere and it's an open avenue for marketing your online business. Social media venues such as Facebook, LinkedIn, Twitter, and Pinterest offer users the ability to specify keywords to target their marketing efforts. Automatically, your ads are being viewed by consumers already interested in what you have to offer. You have now saved money and countless hours of footwork in locating your target audience. While there are some fees involved in promoting or marketing your business through social media, the financial burden is much less than hard copy or printed ads might cost. The business can also control the time of marketing releases to fit their schedule and agenda as opposed to the time constraints associated with print copy.

One major trend is coordinating your business press or marketing releases with what is happening in the world at that particular moment. Because traditional marketing scenarios take time in planning and generating, the moment may be lost in timing. However, the instant publication platform that social media marketing allows, gives you the opportunity to market your business in a timely manner before the moment is lost to an updated news trend. Your online business will soon be perceived as a business that keeps up with the ever changing demands of our world today.

Because you're most likely using these social media outlets for personal reasons, why not begin incorporating the name of your business with your personal information. Most people would prefer to utilize a business they are familiar with on a personal level. This technique offers a feeling of trust and predictability that traditional marketing efforts lack.

When conversations form online and several users who know one another begin to use your name, there is another level of trust that is added to the already familiar business name. This could take months, sometimes years with dated marketing endeavors and your business has managed to produce the same results in a mere fraction of the time it may have taken traditionally.

An important tactic to remember when using social media as your key marketing tool is to become engaged in conversations that involve subjects that target the same issues and ideas that surround your business. Make sure you are participating in conversations by "liking" the points of others within the conversation or contributing positive aspects to the conversation as a mere participant. People have an innate need to be heard and acknowledged. It is extremely important to engage in these online conversations as an interested party and not someone who is simply lurking only to get their business name out there and recognized. Once you have established yourself as a valued participant in conversations, any use of your business name from that point on will be viewed in a more positive light than if you were to use it constantly without invitation or need.

Quality Control

Once your business is recognized on social media outlets you'll want to keep your name associated with positive perceptions by your audience. Even the most successful online businesses have received their fair share of bad publicity or negative comments. Traditional consumers can be leery of online businesses as opposed to store-fronts due to the inability to deal with someone face-to-face. It's important to look at this as an opportunity as opposed to a setback.

Social media has given you a means to address the issue with not only the individual with the complaint but the onlookers who want to know how you resolve dissatisfaction by your consumers. Once again people need to feel acknowledged and validated. That is half the battle in a nutshell. Not only does this simple task defuse a difficult situation, it allows others to see that your business is personal and accountable. We all know that no one is perfect and consumers need businesses to realize that as well.

Once acknowledgment and validation have been offered, you can move on to resolution. This discussion can take place publicly, online, and is invaluable to the business. Consider how many people heard negative things about a business via "word of mouth" but were rarely, if ever, able to witness the resolution. There are cases, however, where the resolution would be better offered privately between the consumer and the business. This can also work to the advantage of the business as it gives the appearance of valuing the disgruntled consumer enough to give them private, personalized attention. Once the consumer is satisfied they're more apt to offer a positive review of your business to those asking about the outcome of the situation during online conversations that will inevitably be taking place.

The Future Of Social Media Marketing

Consumers are now doing everything online from conversing with friends and family to watching movies and keeping up with the news. You can make sure that your business is visible in every online space available for marketing. Social media marketing is a simple tool that will quickly associate your business name with the very people who share an interest in what your business has to offer. Social media marketing is a necessity in today's business world and you can make it work to your advantage by developing your marketing plan utilizing the tools available through social media platforms. The platforms mentioned at the beginning are just a few that are used daily by millions of people.

Start by searching social media sites and make a list of what they offer in terms of marketing. You can then coordinate what is available through social media sites with your marketing agenda and business goals.

You now have the power and control you need to successfully market your business utilizing social media as your platform. New online businesses are continuously being established, and even traditional store-front businesses are incorporating the online business model. It has never been more important for your online business to utilize social media marketing than it is today. The decreased financial burden of social media marketing and the increased viewership of social media marketing strategies are growing quickly and the sooner you incorporate these into your business model the faster your business name will be recognized as a pioneer in social media marketing.

Facebook Marketing for Online Business

With billions of users spanning across all possible demographics, it's a no-brainer for any business enterprise, big or small, to carve a presence on Facebook, the world's biggest social media network. The importance of marketing Facebook leaving a footprint on it has become very critical, so much so that an enterprise that isn't on the site probably does not exist at all.

Consider the ordinary Internet user. A person interested in, say, your business would more likely go to Google to look up information about your business. If yours is linked to Facebook, one of the first things that will show up on the search engine results would be the said Facebook page, followed by the official website of your business. Between the two, the ordinary Internet user is likely to click the one relating to Facebook because, let's face it, Facebook is more familiar. Besides, who has time to navigate through a business website?

It goes without saying, therefore, that insofar as marketing initiatives are concerned, having an organization's presence felt by using Facebook for marketing counts as one of the essential must-do's.

There are plenty of reasons why any marketer worth his salt, or any business enterprise for that matter, should not forego Facebook. Here are some of them:

1. Facebook has over a billion users. Yes, billion.

As the largest and arguably the most influential social media site today, it goes without a surprise that Facebook, a site originally designed for college students, now has over a billion users. These users come from all corners of the world: across geographical boundaries, race, age, gender, social strata, and all possible sorts of inclinations. Facebook's demographics are expansive and cover all possible markets.

This fact alone should be enough reason for any business to do marketing through Facebook. However, the number of people on Facebook should not deceive you into believing that by merely being on the site, success automatically follows. It takes more than that.

If anything, Facebook's popularity is indicative of your potential to find your target market, create a fruitful engagement with them, and harness the social media network's functions to eventually translate these connections into profits.

2. Unless you choose to pay for ads, using Facebook is free.

Traditional marketing strategies that utilize print, TV, and radio cost money. Not with Facebook. Signing up for Facebook only requires a valid email and a phone number for security and you should be all set.

Using Facebook for marketing significantly reduces costs, particularly for businesses with very minimal budget allotted for marketing. As such, it works for small enterprises keen on letting the word out on their business but with little money to spare for advertising. For big businesses, creating a Facebook account serves to strengthen their market hold and support further growth.

3. Facebook provides an array of marketing alternatives.

For the uninitiated, a Facebook page is essentially the business equivalent of a person's status feed. A Facebook page is ordinarily what people look at to get an overview of what your business has been up to. It is free to set up, and only requires imagination and creativity to get it rolling.

But quite apart from pages, Facebook likewise provides two other marketing options: groups and ads on Facebook. A Facebook group can either be public or private. It is different from a page in the sense that a group tends to foster discussions or interactions among its members while a page is generally intended to serve as a repository of updates, promos, and other marketing gimmicks. But similar to pages, groups are also free to set up.

Unlike pages and groups, ads on Facebook are not free; businesses that choose to post ads have to pay, depending on the number of clicks or interactions created by the ad.

Of course, the beauty about marketing Facebook is that the ad is directed to your actual target market. With the vast data Facebook has, advertising on the site means you get to decide which people of a certain age living in a certain place will see your ad. The approach is more direct, hence more effective. Ads on Facebook are also less visually obtrusive; ads are displayed in a manner that does not make them annoying. They are also relevant because they are tailor-fitted according to the profile and stated interests of a certain user.

4. Facebook can rack up traffic to your own site.

Once you have created an audience on Facebook, it now becomes much easier to link up your own website. Many businesses post links on their Facebook pages, groups, or ads enticing their audience to click a link which directs to their own website. It's a nifty way to guarantee an increase in traffic on your own site without coming across as hard sell.

5. Marketing through Facebook promotes a strong feedback mechanism.

The good (or bad) thing about Facebook is that anyone's voice can be heard by merely posting a comment. This is good if you want to have an idea of how your market reacts to your business or an aspect of it. Depending on the kind of feedback, you can either continue doing what your customers love, or devise ways to address concerns raised.

Many times, the comments generated by your Facebook account serve as a springboard for others to post their own comments, too. Positive feedback are almost always seconded by others who have had the same wonderful experience. However, it is the negative comments that mostly stir other people's curiosity. Handling these negative comments in a professional manner is key in turning them into opportunities to shine through.

6. Having an account on Facebook is a great way to earn more leads.

By building a page or running ads on Facebook, you get to expand your potential customers or clients. This becomes even more obvious when you engage in marketing strategies, such as contests and signups, where you get to have the email addresses and phone numbers of these people which they have given voluntarily. These information are crucial for marketing and generating sales outside of Facebook. In this sense, Facebook is useful in enabling you to create leads of who may be interested in your business without bombarding their personal Facebook accounts.

7. And finally, marketing Facebook provides a statistical overview of the performance of your business.

Most of all, Facebook provides an Insights page that allows you as a page owner or advertiser to have a statistical overview of how your page or ad is doing. Facebook's Insights works in the same way as Google's Analytics: Both provide data relating to the number of impressions, clicks, views, likes, and the performance of the pages or ads on Facebook that can be managed to display either a daily, weekly, monthly, or even an annual assessment.

While these figures may seem intimidating at first, knowing what they mean is crucial in understanding how your audience reacts and in determining what strategies work and what don't. They are also important because they serve as a sound basis for whatever changes you seek to implement or initiatives you wish to jumpstart.

Given the foregoing, there is little doubt that Facebook is a great starting point to establish your online business. Needless to say, now is as good a time as any to start using Facebook for marketing.

The Power of Facebook Ads

Nowadays, you will hardly meet anyone not on Facebook. The internet is basically an extended arm of a human that is primarily used to interact with other humans in the cyber world. If you are not on Facebook, there is a high chance that you're missing out on the latest trends, the most controversial political news, and the most scandalous celebrity drama that your friends and family are currently tuned into.

However, you would know by now that Facebook is a very powerful tool and it has more uses than just "poking" a friend and hitting "like" on photos you find on your feed. Small enterprises to large corporations use Facebook as a business tool to promote their company's best interest. With Facebook, different kinds of businesses from different kinds of industries are able to build their brands and reach their target markets; even the most unlikely business, such as a law firm, can invest in Facebook to promote their services.

To be precise, law firms can make use of Facebook Ads to give more attention to their profession. What's good about this is there is an almost-untapped market on Facebook since their competitors are still stuck in the past by putting up physical ads on newspapers and yellow pages or even advertising themselves on TV or radio, which tend to be quite pricey. Little do these firms know, but this form of "traditional" mass advertising does not work well anymore and would actually only reach a small portion of people especially since the global shift on how advertisements is presented –this is where social media, a.k.a. The Internet, comes in the picture.

What's a Facebook ad, anyway? How does it work? According to Facebook, the popular social media network has about two billion active users around the world. That makes it a very attractive advertising platform for users to promote and grow their business. Facebook makes it easy to do so with a few simple steps since the social media page provides user-friendly instructions and illustrations for anyone who wish to make use of Facebook ads.

First, they must choose an objective. For a law firm, that would be to attract new clients by building brand awareness and promoting the specific practice areas that they cater to. Choosing the target audience would be next. Given that facebook has a lot of users, the business must determine the people they want to reach. Facebook allows them to customize the audience by demographics, location, interests, and behavior so they know who to show the ads to. Not only do they show this to your desired audience but also to people similar to them which then increases the chances of reaching other users who may be interested in the business. For a firm, it would be wise to target depending on the specific practice area they handle. A firm that specializes in Corporate Law, for example, targets both the consumers and the working class.

Like any other businesses in the world, a law firm should clearly specify in their ad how they are unique from the rest of their competitors. The ad should answer the question, "Why should we hire you in the first place?" But of course, all law firms would claim that they are the best amongst the rest of the law pool; an ad should be able to catch the attention of their audience at first glance. It has been debated that it would only take about four to six seconds for an ad to catch the attention of a human before they move on to the next bright virtual object that distracts them. Since people have very short attention spans, Facebook adheres to the rule to have ads limit their content to 20% text only; meaning, the rest of the ad should be expressed in a different way —through the use of colors and imagery. This rule actually works wonders for viewers who are always on the go. Even if the audience is willing to take an extra few minutes to do research on law firms on Facebook, the one with the most eye-catching ad that is straight to the point would always be the advantageous one. Having Facebook ads is a powerful tool for growing law firms with aims to expand their horizons, since you'll never know who would be needing legal help. Facebook is a place where all kinds of people from all over the world come together. With this tool, law firms who wish to broaden their scope are able to reach international online traffic with only a click of a button.

For businesses like law firms, using Facebook ads is a cost effective way of advertising for many reasons. The firm can set their budget easily and get their money's worth. Law firms usually rely on mass advertising but they don't really know who sees them or who attracts them. Since Facebook allows users to customize their target audience and to focus on them, the advertisement will not be shown to users who have no interest in their service. More importantly, the firm can gather data to see how well their ad is doing. Facebook provides insights and other tools through the adverts manager to help the business understand their market better and create more effective advertisements.

How to Use Instagram to Market your Online Business

Facebook and Twitter are two of the most popular platforms to advertise your product, but marketing on Instagram is starting to gain ground in the industry. You can boost your online business with your Instagram account. What's with Instagram that makes it a great tool for your business?

One, it is popular. As mentioned, it is one of the most widely-used social media platforms today. Aside from its user-friendly interface, it is fairly easy to create advertisements, memes, and virtual flyers and posters with Instagram.

Marketing on Instagram may be your ticket to fame and success, as many Instagram users are shoppers. The virtual community itself is filled with customers who are eager to see something new in the platform and to share whatever is worth their time and money.

Second, Instagram makes brands accessible, as Facebook and Twitter do. Social media marketing has taken online selling and advertising to new heights. In a study in 2015, it was found out that 70 percent of Instagram users look for a brand in the same platform. Perhaps, this is because these users are visual shoppers and they like seeing new products and promos from the brands they are following.

Images are the strongest motivators to shoppers and looking up the IG accounts and posts of brands is tantamount to online shopping. It can be noted that Instagram helps consumers make smarter decisions, and helps entrepreneurs become better sellers.

Why Instagram?

Instagram is not only popular, but it's also useful and easy to manage. Anyone with a smartphone can download the app from Google Playstore, and the fun starts in minutes. Unlike Facebook, IG is not too strict about photos used in advertisements. Consumers can also scroll through your page and browse more products using their Android phones.
But how do you use social media marketing to boost your business?

The basics: Set up you IG account. This account is for your business and should be separate from your personal interests. Your IG account will target your clients, hence the posts should make them want to see more of your products. Whatever is relevant and meaningful to your customers is what you should focus on. If this means you not appearing on ANY Instagram post, so be it.

Moreover, make sure that the IG account and username match your company's name. The logo of your brand should be the profile picture in your IG account. Because you want to keep the influx of consumers going to your page, being consistent with the profile picture and name will help solidify the consumers' image of your brand. The account name should also be unique.

Second, include a link to attract consumer traffic to your account. The use of hashtags, those phrases and words that are preceded by a number sign (#) can do the trick. When consumers type a certain keyword on the search box, they will be directed to hashtags or links that display the same words. The link may also be your company website. This should be displayed on top of your IG page.

Third, be consistent with the photos. Instagram has the photo filter feature that lets you edit your images. You can play with colors (i.e. make the tone yellowish or sepia) so that the best part of the image is highlighted. A beautifully-written caption should accompany your image. A rule of thumb for businesses is to use the image of a product, a testimonial or a photo of a satisfied customer, and inspirational words that make people think of your products.

Suppose you own a bakeshop, and you want to take photos of your products. You can take advantage of your creativity here. You may emphasize the "Pastry of the Day", showing only one pastry. You may also show a color-coded pastry, for example a treat on Valentine's Day (a slice of red velvet cake, a heart-shaped placemat, and a red mug). You may also use your wit and post a meme that says "How's your bread and butter today?" that can be taken figuratively, but can also be shown as a literal slice of bread with a roll of butter on top. There are so many creative options with Instagram. You only have to think and try what could work for your brand.

Next, write an interesting bio for yourself and an equally interesting description for your brand. This seals the deal with your customers. It's telling them whom they should trust (you) and why they should check out the rest of your photos. Though you can exercise your creative license, you must keep your bio and description light, concise, and to-the-point. You can write about who you are, what you do for a living, and something that would entice readers to buy from you, or at least click the link that you have included.

You may feel proud when people follow your account. It's basically like fangirling. It won't hurt to follow potential customers. Like their photos, especially those that are of the same nature and topic as your business. This is where hashtags come in.

However, Instagram is not the place to do hard-selling. Photos are used creatively to convey images. Sometimes, a text in the image is not necessary, but the careful arrangement of products and other props for your "photo shoot" give your image the " X" factor.

That said, the photos must be of excellent quality – a photo with a high resolution is preferred. It should also be sized properly. The images should also be professional-looking. If possible, images may be edited previously, using more sophisticated and advanced software such as Adobe PowerPoint. Good thing there are apps such as Instasize that can edit the photos quickly.

You may also jumpstart on introducing various promos and announcements in your IG account. Whereas Facebook can upload brochures, flyers, and post longer texts, you have to exercise brevity in Instagram. Again, the image should already speak for the brand, and should promote a positive brand image and culture.

It is likewise important to update your Instagram account often, if not daily. People will always keep an eye on their favorite brands, and they would want to be the first to know if the company has released a new product or promo. Use this 'proactive' attitude in social media shopping to your advantage. You can balance out all the fun and professionalism in your posts. Tell a story with a single picture. Use drama to appeal to the consumers' emotions and logic.

What's good about IG is that it can be connected to Facebook and Twitter. Thus, you can target three social media accounts with just one post. This online marketing strategy is definitely cost-effective and time-saving. You may also post videos on IG now. Shoppers would like to watch demonstrations and testimonials on videos.

If you can, follow back your followers and comment on their photos. If they took photos of your products and linked you to it, return the favor by saying thank you or providing a feedback of appreciation.

The Future of Your Business with Instagram

With more millennials and digital natives forming a huge percentage of consumers, you can only assume that your business may flourish with IG. You have the power to convince your customers to check out your stuff and eventually buy them. IG is a great social media platform to use for your online business. Because everything is so advanced now, it is only a matter of time before Instagram introduces other cool features aside from image resize and photo filters. Instagram is here to stay.

9

Lifestyle Design

The Concept of Lifestyle Design

The Purpose of Living

Do you want to know what lifestyle design is? To do that start by imagining yourself living the life you have always wanted. Doing the things you have always dreamed of when you were a kid? Then, focus on your life right now and start asking serious questions, such as:

1. Are you living the kind of life you dreamed of when you were little?

2. What happened along the way?

3. What makes you happy?

4. What do you love doing?

5. Why are you not living your ideal life yet?

6. What is stopping you from making that leap of faith?

It's likely though, that you are looking for answers and you feel stuck. Count yourself among those who are not getting any fulfillment with the work they are doing. Somewhere along the way, reality hit you hard in the face. As some say, idealists have no place in this world.

You had to find a job. You had to get married early. You had to work to finance the expenses associated with starting a family. You need to buy the biggest house you can afford and, maybe, a car or two. You take vacations at luxurious destinations at least twice a year. This is the "Great American Dream." However, it's not unlikely that you aspired for something a bit different. What if your idea of happiness lies in doing what you love all the days of your life, and that excludes having a boring desk job? Welcome to the newest concept in town that might have the answers you are looking for: lifestyle design.

The Key Idea of Design

The concept has been around for ages. For many years, people have talked about living a lifestyle that is different from what society expects of its citizens. The concept had just been properly labelled when Timothy Feriss published a book entitled, "The 4-Hour Work Week: Escape 9-5, Live Anywhere, and Join the New Rich" in 2007.

The idea behind lifestyle design is to live the unconventional life. Instead of spending your day at your cubicle doing menial or unfulfilling work, you do meaningful tasks – preferably, at an exotic location. Think of it this way: you travel and experience new things while you are earning enough money, doing jobs that create an impact on the greater majority.

That is as idealistic as it can get, but it is slowly becoming the trend nowadays. This means people are getting tired of living a routine each day and conforming to societal expectations. They are looking for new ways to live their life and to the find meaning of their own destinies.

Is the Concept for You?

The answer's both "yes" and "no". The concept's suitability depends on how you think about certain things in life. If you have no trouble accepting the status quo and its expectations, then maybe you are living the life you actually wanted in the first place. You crave security and stability.

If you desire for something greater than the routine of a life you are living, then lifestyle design is for you. Actually, the idea is not really exotic in itself. It basically means to put your life into your own hands and start calling the shots yourself.

It is all about finding what will make you happy. If that's about staying in the office and being part of a corporate organization, then let it be. If your idea of happiness lies in building a business of your own or spending your time in a faraway land, then so be it. What matters most is that you choose to live your own life according to your own terms.

Chase after What You Want

Identify Your Desires

You need to take a step back and rechannel your focus. If you have been an employee for years now, you will find out that the change is going to have a big impact on your life. Changing your current lifestyle into a completely different one is not a decision that you could make overnight. The lifestyle shift needs a series of planning, preparation, and careful execution, so that you wouldn't find yourself struggling in the mud once you decide to take the plunge.

The first thing you need to do is to find out your inner purpose. That includes knowing what makes you happy, what makes you fulfilled, and what makes you want to add value to the world.

If you have always thought of building your own business empire from scratch, then your purpose is to lead and to achieve. Others find solace in silence and taking the life of poverty. Their main purpose in life is to understand the world.

Find your own voice. It is a surprising fact that most people zip through life, following routines and daily schedules, without knowing the very things they want to do. You can pay attention to your interests, hobbies, and personality traits to arrive at a definite life path that will suit your liking.

Identify What You Are Good At

Many people want to become rock stars, actors, and writers. The problem lies in knowing what you want and finding a skill that is related to your desires. If you want to achieve happiness and success in your life, you have to listen to your inner instincts. Find your strengths, and use them to your advantage.

You have already arrived at a definite purpose. If your desire is to sing and to entertain people, then your skill sets should include a talent in singing and making people laugh. Otherwise, what you want is a hobby. Your needs right now must be applicable to your long-term plans, and that means making a career out of something that drives your passion. That is the main reason why you should capitalize, at least, on something that makes full use of your talents.

Find a Way to Get to Your Dreams

This is the tricky part. Many people have successfully lived with their purposes in mind. These are the ones who made the headlines, published books, and became millionaires doing their thing. These are the people who have made it. However, before all the success, there were stories of failure. It is an inevitable part of life. However, that should not stop you from trying.

Finding the balance between your desires and your strong skills will definitely come as a challenge. You will have to be a resilient individual, one who quickly adapts to changes. In the world of the unconventional lifestyle, every day presents an unpredictable opportunity. You have to find the ones you know will help you advance towards the path you desire.

How do you do this? First, be focused and find areas for growth. Do not allow hesitations to form and develop, just go with the flow and trust in all the possibilities. If you aspire to be a teacher and an opportunity to become a tutor (or a teaching aid) comes, then grab it at once. Soak up every knowledge you'd encounter – or in other words, be open to new ideas.

Second, learn to adapt to change. The unconventional way of living is the least secure path to take. So, expect problems to come. There would be many times when you will not get your way, so just remain patient. Always be calm. Be an optimist, and keep pushing until you get your plans into action.

The Choice of Unconventional Living

Your idea of an unconventional lifestyle may not be as radical as spending the remaining years of your life overseas. You may stay at your home country and still face an itch for something as exciting as change. Even so, you are still bound to face difficulties in the presence of your family, your peers, and the system itself.

Here are some common scenarios, which might help you identify what you want. The life design you will make for yourself may contain one, two, or all of these choices.

1. A Change in Career

Your current job may be earning you plenty of money, but you still cannot ignore the emptiness you are going through. You crave for something new, and you want to shift into a different career (which you think is more suitable to your skills, talents, and interests). Income is one thing, but your happiness is not something you should sacrifice in exchange of a big paycheck.

2. Moving Abroad

Moving to a foreign land with no family and friends is a big decision. It is a challenge that you will face on your own, should you continue your choice. However, going out of your comfort zone will also force you to open your mind to different notions. You will meet new people, hopefully have new friends, and understand the way people live on the opposite part of the continent.

3. Being Your Own Boss

Maybe your purpose lies in being a maker of things. The call of self-employment is an attractive one as you get to handle your own time, be closer to family and friends, watch the world go by, and decide in your own terms. However, expect a bumpy ride ahead. There would be months of struggle, as you start your own firm and as you adjust to being your own employer. In exchange of the risk, you will learn how to be a one-man team and how to manage your time and efforts well.

4. Traveling

Traveling is always an exciting path. You get to see different cultures, and have a deeper understanding of how the world works. This is a better choice to make if you want to explore different countries and visit unexplored territories without having to completely abandon the life you have been born into.

5. Defying Norms and Traditions

There are norms and traditions that do not hold as much value today as they did before. A common example is marriage. Women may now choose to skip marriage, or to delay it to an older age. Gender identity also comes into play, as marriage is no longer for a man and a woman only.

The best decision to make is the one you think would best make you happy. Do not go with tradition if you think it would not be in line with your personal goals and possible lifestyle.

Keep Your Head High

Naysayers will come and go. There is no escape from them, especially not if you are dreaming of living a not-so-ordinary lifestyle. At the end of the day, it is up to you to shape life according to how you see fit. Making a lifestyle plan that is relevant to your beliefs, values, skills, talents, and interests will definitely spell a life of happiness and, eventually, success. Just be sure to go with your decisions and live life with no regrets.

Change and Improve Your Life

Refocus Your Efforts

The life-changing concept was built to force a full-degree turn in one's life. That is why it is not for everyone. This is the reason why it is unconventional. That's also the reason why it is scary and definitely not for the faint of heart.

It is almost akin to throwing your past life away in order to make room for a new one. Imagine yourself spending years in a corporate job while continuously dreaming for a long weekend at the beach. To make every day as if it is a weekend, you'd have to make changes – starting with your job. You need to refocus your efforts to follow the lifestyle you designed for yourself.

You have to start again. The life you once knew as a 9-to-5 employee would be a thing of the past. If this scares you enough, then you know you are aiming for something bigger than you have ever imagined.

A design that goes through the unbeaten path is worthy of note. Not everyone has the courage to make the change, so praise yourself for making a risky decision. The change will be hard at first, but you will like it afterwards. Refocus your efforts into something greater and the universe will reward you for the risk that you took.

Be a Bit Selfish

Following the status quo means you have to always think of others before you act. That is why traditions are made. This view in particular is not bad per se. In fact, it is an altruistic perspective. However, you should also prioritize your needs and wants over those of others, so that you would have a happy life yourself.

When you give and offer every time, you wouldn't learn to love yourself in the long term. You owe to yourself the need to be happy, and you could only do that by listening to your inner desires and making them come true.

It is also impossible to give when you have nothing left. A proper design puts you in the spotlight – going with what you want. If life is a stage, then you are the actor. Be a little selfish by fulfilling your needs first. Once you have become a well-rounded individual, it is now time to give back and help others.

Give Back to the Community

The lifestyle design improves people's lives in a way that individuals who were crazy enough to shake things up also made an impact in the lives of the greater majority. For example, if you have spent so much time listening to your own thoughts, then you will become a matured individual and eventually be a good listener.

You might also notice how those who succeeded in pursuing their passion are the ones who were able to inspire change in different ways. The tech billionaire Bill Gates followed an unconventional lifestyle concept by pursuing his dreams in computer programming. He eventually opened his own multimillion-dollar company, which is now known as the Microsoft Corporation. Currently, he is donating billions to various charitable causes around the world.

If that is not enough proof how a good lifestyle plan is able to help other people, then consider the life and creation of Mark Zuckerberg. He is the brains (and brawn) behind the highly successful social networking site, Facebook. Zuckerberg was able to change modern life by creating a site on which people can easily reach out to others. Because of this invention, it has now become easier to talk to people and stay updated.

Push Your Limits

The only thing to do to become great at something is to take a risk in life. Lifestyle design helps people become creative, innovative, and forward thinking. Since the implementation of the concept results into a complete 360-degree turn (from one kind of life to another), you will be forced to make changes and incorporate new ideas. This will inevitably lead to you discovering your limits – pushing existing boundaries and developing new strengths.

This is just one of the benefits linked in following the unconventional lifestyle. You will also raise your standards for excellence, get to know yourself much more, and become better at what you do. Pushing your limits to the maximum is a great way to invent new things and systems that could potentially add value to the world and to humanity.

Idealists have a separate strength of their own. They believe in the good ideas, the rosy perspectives, and the optimist outlooks. If you condition yourself that there is no limit to what your abilities can achieve, then you become capable of doing so much more than you know you could.

Practice Mindfulness

Following a life-changing notion is all about adopting an idealistic approach to living. In the fast world that many live in now, that is not such a bad thing. Sometimes, all people need is quiet, so they can enjoy their lives better. The trouble with following the rules is that you are restricted in terms of what you could do. The trouble with following schedules is that you are not free to do as you wish.

Months and years could pass by, yet you do not have clear memories as to what happened in between. You are usually just "fast forwarding" and then, eventually, you wake up old and devoid of the time and energy needed to enjoy living.

One of the things that a good design gives is clarity and mindfulness when it comes to the present. Most people nowadays are either stuck in the past or anxious of the future. However, if you decide to go the uncharted route, then you will feel more alive and more appreciative of what you have.

You will get to enjoy time, freedom, and social engagement. More than that, you will have more choices. You will live with purpose, and you'll satisfy your thirst for meaning.

Pay Attention to What Really Matters

The age-old question asks: what is the meaning of life? Is it for fun and pleasure only? The answer's "no". Countless issues in the world need to be solved. Is life for happiness? To a certain extent, since one of the key goals in living is to be happy and to make wonderful memories.

Life is created for a purpose. Each person has a different purpose that's waiting to be discovered firsthand. The life-altering concept can help people become acquainted with their inner desires and turn their purposes into reality. The sooner you'd know what destiny really is, the quicker you'll learn how to control your life and bring change to the world.

To do that, you'd have to pay attention to what really matters – people, causes, ideas, and universal goodness. You only have one life, so make the most of it. Create your own lifestyle design and start taking charge of your own destiny.

Conclusion

The rewards given by entrepreneurship are tremendous. Those who want to attain a great level of freedom without fear of risks are the types who are most likely to succeed in this special lifestyle and vocation.

We have enumerated all the skills of a good entrepreneur - Creativity, marketing, leadership, product value and ethical standards. These are the skills that make up a good leader. Without one of these, success of the business is difficult to achieve.

The next step now is for you to change how you view yourself as an entrepreneur. If you think you lack one of the 5 skills, then I recommend that you start cultivating it now. Those 5 skills can be learned. You can enhance and strengthen them so if you lack one of the mentioned skills, don't worry because you will eventually develop it.

I also shared with you some ideas on how to get started as an entrepreneur. These ideas are simple and anyone with a bit of discipline and focus can start making money within a few weeks. It is up to you to make a choice to take action.

Lastly, I shared with you the idea of lifestyle design. Lifestyle design and entrepreneurship is something that goes hand in hand. Combining the two is something that in the modern world is possible. With the internet, we now can design the way we want to live. This is of course only possible with hard work and perseverance.

CONCLUSION

If you believe that you are ready to start your business and if you are confident that you can be a good entrepreneur, I congratulate you. You may now proceed and contribute in making the world a better place.

Good Luck

Copyright 2019 by John Winters - All rights reserved.

This document is geared towards providing exact and reliable information in regards to the topic and issue covered. The publication is sold with the idea that the publisher is not required to render accounting, officially permitted, or otherwise, qualified services. If advice is necessary, legal or professional, a practiced individual in the profession should be ordered.

- From a Declaration of Principles which was accepted and approved equally by a Committee of the American Bar Association and a Committee of Publishers and Associations.

In no way is it legal to reproduce, duplicate, or transmit any part of this document in either electronic means or in printed format. Recording of this publication is strictly prohibited and any storage of this document is not allowed unless with written permission from the publisher. All rights reserved.

The information provided herein is stated to be truthful and consistent, in that any liability, in terms of inattention or otherwise, by any usage or abuse of any policies, processes, or directions contained within is the solitary and utter responsibility of the recipient reader. Under no circumstances will any legal responsibility or blame be held against the publisher for any reparation, damages, or monetary loss due to the information herein, either directly or indirectly.

Respective authors own all copyrights not held by the publisher.

The information herein is offered for informational purposes solely, and is universal as so. The presentation of the information is without contract or any type of guarantee assurance.

The trademarks that are used are without any consent, and the publication of the trademark is without permission or backing by the trademark owner. All trademarks and brands within this book are for clarifying purposes only and are the owned by the owners themselves, not affiliated with this document.

www.ingramcontent.com/pod-product-compliance
Lightning Source LLC
Chambersburg PA
CBHW021832170526
45157CB00007B/2774